LEADERSHIP
What Every Leader
Should Know About People

Robert A. Portnoy, Ph.D.

Administrator, Human Resources Development
McDonnell Douglas Astronautics Company

D0145659

Prentice-Hall, Inc., *Englewood Cliffs, New Jersey 07632*

Library of Congress Cataloging-in-Publication Data

PORTNOY.
    Leadership: what every leader should know about
people.

    Bibliography: p.
    Includes index.
    1. Executive ability.   2. Leadership.
3. Communication in organizations.   I. Title.
HD38.2.P67 1986   658.4'092   85-19256
ISBN   0-13-526948-2

Editorial/production supervision and
    interior design: Jeanne Hoeting and Mary Bardoni
Cover design: Photo Plus Art
Manufacturing buyer: John B. Hall

Printed in the United States of America

10 9 8 7 6 5 4 3 2 1

ISBN 0-13-526948-2   01

PRENTICE-HALL INTERNATIONAL (UK) LIMITED, *London*
PRENTICE-HALL OF AUSTRALIA PTY. LIMITED, *Sydney*
PRENTICE-HALL CANADA INC., *Toronto*
PRENTICE-HALL HISPANOAMERICANA, S.A., *Mexico*
PRENTICE-HALL OF INDIA PRIVATE LIMITED, *New Delhi*
PRENTICE-HALL OF JAPAN, INC., *Tokyo*
PRENTICE-HALL OF SOUTHEAST ASIA PTE. LTD., *Singapore*
EDITORA PRENTICE-HALL DO BRASIL, LTDA., *Rio de Janeiro*
WHITEHALL BOOKS LIMITED, *Wellington, New Zealand*

CONTENTS

FOREWORD   **ix**

PREFACE   **xi**

Chapter One

TRAINING LEADERS TO WORK WITH PEOPLE   **1**

Major Concepts   2
Introduction   2
Leadership Means Business   3
Definitions of Leadership and Management   4

Organization   4
Organizational Resources   5
The Decisive Function   5
The Directive Function   5
The Representative Function   6
Authority   6

Management   12
Leadership   13

Structured Training in Leadership   14
Rationale For People Study in Leadership   15
Important People Skills of Top Executives   16
A Necessary Component for Effective Leadership   20
Summary   20
Topics for Discussion   20
Recommended Readings   21

Chapter Two

THE MECHANISMS OF HUMAN BEHAVIOR   23

Major Concepts   24
Introduction   25
The Relationship Life Cycle   25

Credibility   26
Becoming Acquainted   27
Forming Attachments   28
Defining Expectations and Role Clarification   29
Integration and Commitment   31
Stability   32
Jolts   33
Instability   35
Eroded Commitment   37
Disintegration   39
Adaptation to Change   39

The Behavior Operating System   42

Homeostatic Programming   43
The Dynamic Framework of Personality   43
The Disruption of Rational Thinking   46
A Case of Domestic Conflict   49
An Analysis of the Case Study   53

Summary   54
Topics for Discussion   56
Recommended Readings   56

Chapter Three

EMOTIONAL STABILITY IN LEADERSHIP   57

Major Concepts   58
Introduction   59

The Case of Dr. Kramer   60

Analysis of the Case Study   66
The Identification and Management of Superego
    Triggers   66

Time Management   67
Physical Activity   73
Relaxation   75

Summary   79
Topics for Discussion   79
Recommended Readings   80

Chapter Four

BASIC COMMUNICATION SKILLS   81

Major Concepts   82
Introduction   82
Basic Communication Skills   83

Conversation   83
Assertiveness   85
Confrontation   87
Feedback   92
Dealing with Criticism   97

Summary   98
Topics for Discussion   99
Recommended Readings   99

Chapter Five

APPLIED COMMUNICATION:
DIRECTIONS AND POLICIES   101

Major Concepts   102
Introduction   103
Setting the Agenda   103

The Formal Agenda   104
The Informal Agenda   106

Speaking Before A Group   108
Giving Directions   110
Announcing Policies   111
Managing Interruptions   112
Decision Making   114

Arbitration   115
Team Decision Making   116

Consequences for Unsatisfactory Performance   122
Summary   123
Topics for Discussion   124
Recommended Readings   124

Chapter Six

CASE STUDIES: PROBLEMS AND SOLUTIONS   125

Introduction   126
The Case of Tom Demerist   127

The Problem   127
The Solution   133

The Case of Beverly Jacoby   139

The Problem   139
The Solution   142

The Case of Jerry Williams   147

The Problem   147
The Solution   151

Summary   154
Topics for Discussion   154

Chapter Seven

SUMMARY   157

Overview   158
Questions and Answers   160
Final Examination   169

APPENDIX 175

Appendix A: The Job-List Binder Form   177
Appendix B: The Response-Time Binder Form   179
Appendix C: Final Examination—Answer Key   181

REFERENCES 183

INDEX 187

FOREWORD

American businesses collectively spend over 3 billion dollars per year to improve the effectiveness of supervisors and managers. There are serious questions about the success of much of this effort. Too many of the training models focus on trying to develop idealized leadership traits in leadership trainees. The hard lesson learned is simply that charm, charisma, and a magnetic personality are characteristics of particular people who seem to have natural tendencies as born leaders. These characteristics have been wrongly considered to be the same as supervisory or management skills. In other words, trainers have reasoned that if a supervisor could learn how to be more charismatic, that person would also become more effective. In reality, trying to teach charisma to a non-charismatic person is as futile as teaching music appreciation to someone who is tone deaf.

There is no doubt, however, that effective training can enhance the productivity of many supervisors and managers. But since previous attempts to prepare supervisors and managers for leadership have been disappointing, we must ask ourselves how leadership training programs can be made more effective. *Leadership: What Every Leader Should Know About People* is an interesting and fresh approach to this question.

This book is a complete training program for both the new and experienced supervisor or manager. The skills that it teaches are consistent with common sense. They are natural skills, relatively easy to apply, and they explain a great deal about human behavior. The book, moreover, is filled with lively case studies and provocative discussion. As a training manual, this work is systematically structured for the reader who is committed to intensive study and rigorous application.

As an executive, I have worked with a number of leaders from across the world. In my mind, what distinguished the great leaders was how well they had developed the skills to motivate people. No book could by itself establish those skills for anyone. However, this book puts the focus of training leaders where it should be—on understanding the nature of the people to be led so that their behavior can be firmly guided into productive channels.

George S. Graff

Past President—McDonnell Aircraft Company
Member, Board of Directors
McDonnell Douglas Corporation

PREFACE

This book is about people. It is based on the notion that a leader's effectiveness depends upon the capacity to influence, motivate, and cooperate with people. Research has established that a leader's success relates more with learning these kinds of "people" skills than it does with innate abilities in the areas of charm, magnetism, and charisma.

In this book can be found both theory and technique on leadership. One theory attempts to explain how a working relationship develops and either adapts to the changing needs of its members or disintegrates as relentless conflicts erode both interpersonal and organizational commitment. A second theory discusses how human temperament can be used as a knowledge base to logically explain, predict, and modify the impulsive behaviors that can interfere with the achievement of organizational objectives. Based on these theoretical platforms, practical techniques will be offered that enhance a leader's abilities in giving meaning and direction to the work of people within an organization.

I would like to thank several people for their help and support in the preparation of this manuscript. Gary Sudin provided the technical knowledge and support I needed to produce the manuscript through electronic media. Sister Marie Damien Adams, Sister Jane Hassett, Dr.

Janie von Wolfseck, and Ms. Vivian Schoeck provided constant enthusiasm at times when I thought my own reserves would buckle. My sister, Julie Greskamp, provided the inspiration that my mother didn't have the opportunity to send firsthand. My children Annie and Benjy always gave me a bedtime smile that helped me keep working long past the time I tucked them in. And my wife Lisa has made everything I try to do worthwhile. Thank you.

Robert A. Portnoy

CHAPTER ONE
TRAINING LEADERS
TO WORK WITH PEOPLE

OUTLINE

MAJOR CONCEPTS
INTRODUCTION
LEADERSHIP MEANS BUSINESS
CONCEPTUAL DEFINITIONS OF LEADERSHIP AND MANAGEMENT

    Organization
    Organizational Resources
    The Decisive Function
    The Directive Function
    The Representative Function
    Authority
    Management
    Leadership

STRUCTURED TRAINING IN LEADERSHIP
RATIONALE FOR PEOPLE STUDY IN LEADERSHIP
IMPORTANT PEOPLE SKILLS OF TOP EXECUTIVES
A NECESSARY COMPONENT FOR EFFECTIVE LEADERSHIP
SUMMARY
TOPICS FOR DISCUSSION
RECOMMENDED READINGS

MAJOR CONCEPTS

1. The need to formally train supervisors, managers, and business owners in the principles of leadership is becoming recognized as an economic necessity by American industry.
2. A *leader* is a person who has the authority to decide, direct, and represent the objectives and functions of an organization.
3. A *manager* is a person who has the authority to direct specific organizational resources in order to accomplish objectives.
4. *Authority* is the license by an organization that grants an individual the rights to use its powers and resources.
5. *Credibility* is the recognition by an organization that one is competent to use its powers.
6. *Technical credibility* is established when the organization believes that an individual is competent in areas of technical specialization.
7. *Ethical credibility* is established when the organization believes that an individual will uphold and support the ethical standards of the organization.
8. *Interpersonal credibility* is established when the personnel within the organization believe that an individual understands and cares about what happens to them.
9. The problem of poorly prepared leaders relates more to the nature of leadership training that has been available than to the actual number of training programs.
10. The actual traits of the leader's personality appear to be less important than the skills that the leader uses to influence and motivate the people who follow.
11. Leadership skills involve redirecting human behavior from impulsive and self-serving actions into productive channels that can benefit both the worker as well as the organization.
12. The definition of an organization is a body made up of parts that are dependent on one another while at the same time each has its own special function.

INTRODUCTION

When I was 6 years old, my father gave me a plastic model airplane kit. When I opened the box I found a number of unassembled pieces, assorted decals, a tube of glue, and a set of directions. Since my reading skills were at the Dick and Jane level, I concluded that the directions would be of little use to me so I set them aside. I proceeded to assemble the model airplane using what resources I did have available to me: namely, the picture of the plane on the box, my assumptions about how the pieces should fit together, and my determination to get finished with the assembly so that I could go on combat missions in my mother's living room. Sure enough, despite the globs of glue between my fingers, I succeeded.

After a number of years had passed, along with countless bombing raids over the dining room table, my father gave me my first set of tools. Unlike the model airplane kit, the tools did not come with a set of directions. Of course, any kid knew what to do with a screwdriver, hammer, saw, and pliers. Who needed directions? It was a particularly good time for me to get these tools considering that my clock radio recently stopped working. Since I had been so skillful at assembling all those model airplanes, and knew all about tools, fixing the radio would be a piece of cake. The clock itself still functioned, which told me that the problem must be with one of the tubes housed deep within the radio itself. I carefully removed each one of the screws from the back panel. This panel bears that ominous-looking *Caution* phrase warning unskilled hands not to tamper with the insides of a radio. As with the directions from the model airplane kit, I set the panel aside. Then peering into the depths of the radio to find an array of tubes, colored wires, soldered connections, and otherwise unidentifiable parts, I reached around to the front and turned the radio on, waiting to see which of the tubes lit up. The culprit would, of course, remain dark; then it would simply be a matter of replacing it with a new tube. To my surprise, they all lit up. Now what? I picked up the rubber-tipped screwdriver and the bare metal pliers to gently tug at wires, hoping to find a short. Apparently I found it. The next thing I knew, I had been knocked on my back in a puff of blue smoke amid the crackling of shooting white sparks and the acrid smell of burning rubber wires. My elevation from the ranks of model plane assembler to radio repairman reached an abrupt and humiliating end.

Like the precocious child, most people who reach positions of leadership are bright, determined, and energetic. But just like that precocious child, many lack the necessary training and direction that is so essential in guiding them toward success. And without this training, despite all the creativity and hard work, they and their businesses could come to an abrupt and humiliating end.

LEADERSHIP MEANS BUSINESS

For the majority of people, leadership does not come naturally. There are many instances in which ill-prepared individuals suddenly become saddled with the responsibilities of leadership. Businesses sometimes promote workers who are unqualified for leadership to administrative positions as a form of recognition for a job well done. Civic groups may draft members into leadership roles because of their contributions to community service. All too often, these new supervisors, managers, and chapter officers find themselves at a loss when faced with the pressures and responsibilities of their leadership roles.

The need to formally train supervisors, managers, and business owners in the principles of leadership is becoming recognized as an economic necessity by American industry. In 1981, the rate of business failures in the United States reached a record high of 16,800. This figure represents a progressive increase of 250 percent in the number of businesses that have failed since 1978 (Bureau of the Census, 1982–1983).

The roots of business failure can often be traced in part to inadequate training among business leaders. Research spanning the last three decades reveals the growing disenchantment of American business with the graduates of business schools (Gorden & Howell, 1959; Livingston, 1971; Mahmoud & Frampton, 1975; *Business Week*, 1980; Pollack et al., 1983; and Hoy & Boulton, 1983). The higher centers of learning are simply not preparing students to meet the changing and challenging needs of today's business world (Prentice, 1983). The area of knowledge that both employers and students alike agree is a necessity in preparing the student to meet these demands is that of leadership.

CONCEPTUAL DEFINITIONS OF LEADERSHIP AND MANAGEMENT

A *leader* is an individual who has the authority to decide, direct, and represent the objectives and functions of an organization. A *manager* is an individual who has the authority to direct specific organizational resources in order to accomplish objectives. Each definition is based on at least three separate concepts. To help you better understand the definitions, let's take a look at each concept separately. Then, we will reintegrate them to consider how they give meaning to both definitions.

Organization

The definition of an organization is a body made up of parts that are dependent on one another while at the same time each has its own special function (Prentice, 1983). In other words, in an organization the parts work together to achieve a common goal. Organizational behavior is directed toward cooperative achievement rather than individual accomplishment. The organization may recognize individuality, but usually only in so far as the results contribute to what the organization desires.

The objectives of the organization pertain to the results it hopes to accomplish. The functions include the plans for accomplishing those objectives as well as the actual procedures and policies that will hopefully produce the desired results. As an analogy consider the objectives to be a destination, perhaps like a city, whereas the functions are like landmarks on a roadmap—they provide the opportunities for getting where the organization wants to go. From the organization's point of view, "the functions are what we do and the objectives are why we do them."

Organizational Resources

An organization's resources are the tools it has available in order to carry out its work. These resources generally include a building with areas for work and for storage, materials, and equipment; an operating budget for the expenditure of money; an operating budget for the expenditure of time; and, of course, human resources to plan and perform the work. To continue with our analogy, if a destination is like an organization's objective and a roadmap is like the plan, then a car, fuel, and a driver would be like the resources.

The Decisive Function

The people who are in charge of the organization routinely scrutinize its reason for existence to determine if the benefits of existence outweigh the costs. These people are the ones who steer the organization along its course. Based on their insights, their wisdom, their experience, and sometimes their whims and impulses, they may shift that course, alter the objectives, and consequently radically or completely change the organizational policies, functions, and resources. They must examine the past in order to justify the present and to determine the future of the organization.

The Directive Function

The organization depends upon certain of its personnel to see that its plans are put into action so that its objectives can be accomplished. The directive function incorporates the use of power so that the directing personnel can put the organization's resources to work. A directive from a superior is that form of power that can put human resources into operation. Through these directives, the subordinates work to accomplish specific tasks that in turn will accomplish the organization's objectives.

The Representative Function

The organization exists as a single entity. However, it does not exist in isolation. It may be part of a community, an industry, and a society. Just as the individual parts make up the whole of the organization, so too does the organization belong to a larger sphere. For example, an automobile manufacturing company is held accountable by the U.S. government to protect the American consumer against safety hazards. As another example, a private college may conduct a capital fundraising drive in its home community in order to keep its doors open to students.

In each case, the organization must designate someone to represent its interests to that larger sphere. The members of that larger sphere will likely view the representative as though that person and the organization were one and the same.

Authority

To review up to this point, a leader is an individual who has the authority to decide, direct, and represent the objectives and functions of an organization. A manager is an individual who has the authority to direct specific organizational resources in order to accomplish objectives. We have examined each of the concepts mentioned in both the definitions of leadership and management except that of authority. In many ways the concept of authority, as compared with the others, is the most complex. Accordingly, it warrants considerably more discussion.

It is important to begin a discussion of authority by showing how it differs from power. Operationally defined, *power* is a force by which to accomplish objectives. That force could be in the form of a fuel such as gasoline, an implement such as a piece of equipment, or a human resource such as knowledge. For example, a construction company that uses a crane to hoist materials needs several forms of power: the fuel to power the crane, the crane itself to lift materials, and the human operator who has the know-how to operate it. Without any one of the three forms of power the materials could not be hoisted, at least not in as efficient a manner.

As differentiated from power, *authority* represents the permission or license to use the power. For example, the crane operator likely has the authority to use the crane on the construction site, during normal working hours, and only for the purpose for which it was intended. The operator, even though having the power (that is, knowledge and perhaps even the ignition keys) to use the crane, does not have the authority to use it off of the site, outside of normal working hours, or for purposes other than that for which it was intended. As another example, a credit card represents buying power. By definition, it too is a force by which to accomplish objectives. News reports have recently disclosed that certain people have searched the trash bins of stores for discarded carbons that contain the card numbers of credit card owners. These individuals use the numbers to make unauthorized purchases. In other words, they have power without authority.

In order for an organization to entrust an individual with its powers, it must be convinced that the person has the knowledge and skill to use those powers. This process of so convincing the organization of one's competence is called *credibility*. Three forms of credibility are technical, ethical, and interpersonal.

Technical credibility.   Technical credibility is one of the three avenues through which one can gain recognition as authority. Individuals attempt to establish technical credibility by convincing an organization that they can effectively direct its resources so that its objectives will be accomplished.

As an example, a pharmaceutical manufacturing firm would hire a research chemist based on her academic credentials, references, professional publications, and interviewing skills. In this manner, she has convinced the firm that she is technically credible. Whether or not she will actually be able to perform the work according to the firm's expectations will depend upon the way in which her abilities mesh with the responsibilities of the job itself. Nonetheless, once the organization accepts her technical credibility, it will entrust her with a certain degree of power. These powers might include keys to buildings, secret formulas, the use of its company letterhead for correspondence, and so forth. What has been established, therefore, is her technical credibility. In short, the firm believes in her.

Technical credibility, in other words, is recognition for abilities that are assumed to be present. Technical *competence* is the type and amount of ability that an individual actually possesses. Either may be present without the other. An incompetent person could be given a position because of whom he knows rather than what he knows (credibility without competence), whereas a highly skilled person might be overlooked if his image is inconsistent with the organization's expectations (competence without credibility).

Technical competence includes at least two categories of skills. The first form is called "specialty skills." It relates to the area of expertise that the individual has developed to prepare for his career specialty. A physician, for example, is technically competent to practice medicine, an attorney has developed knowledge and skills for the practice of the law, and a professional salesperson has been thoroughly trained for the product he represents as well as for the market for which it is most directly targeted. This form of technical competence specifically qualifies the individual to engage in the practice of a career, or at least to perform certain job functions.

An individual could, of course, have become technically competent in specialty skills without having developed the competence to direct human resources. This second form of technical competence is called "directive skills." As previously discussed, the organization depends upon certain of its personnel to see that its plans are put into action so that its objectives can be accomplished. The directive function incorporates the use of power so that the directing personnel can put the organization's resources to work. Through these directives, the subordinates work to accomplish specific tasks by which they will accomplish the organization's objectives.

The directive skills involve the performance of five specific procedures: (1) setting task objectives, (2) organizing work, (3) motivating workers, (4) measuring performance, and (5) increasing the competence of workers to perform tasks efficiently and productively (Drucker, 1973). Each procedure has its own beginning and ending; when the first ends, the second one begins. The complexities are divided up into a number of smaller units so that each can be accomplished in its own alotted time; one right after another. Together, the tasks make up a logical sequence that fit within a work cycle (Wilson, 1979).

Goal Setting and Clarification. The first step in any kind of work is to set goals and objectives. The work director must be clear as to exactly what is to be accomplished. Next, the workers must be helped to understand what needs to be accomplished and in what ways achieving the goal will benefit not only the company, but also themselves.

Planning and Problem Solving. The planning will necessarily include specifications as to the amount of time to be allotted, the type and number of personnel that will be required, how much money will be needed, and so on. In addition, this task requires the planning team to anticipate problems that may arise so that contingency plans can be developed and made ready.

Work Facilitation. After the work itself is planned, specific instructions must be delivered to all of the members of the work team. The work director then supports that work with all of the necessary resources. The support may call for allocating funds, ordering materials, establishing channels for delegation, and specialized training to minimize or prevent potential difficulties. Above all, the work director's role is to support the process through whatever assistance and resources can be reasonably made available.

Obtaining and Providing Feedback. This task involves determining the ways in which the work team is progressing toward the goal. In addition, the work director informs each of the workers how he or she is assessing their efforts.

Making Control Adjustments. The work director must institute the appropriate changes. These adjustments may involve reinstructing people, improving work facilitation, allocating additional funds, hiring supplementary personnel, or perhaps even removing particular personnel from the project itself. Careful consideration of the circumstances might even dictate that the goal itself must be revised.

These directive skills are, in other words, power that an individual needs in order to direct human resources. Through the company's belief in this technical competence, individuals can establish technical credibility; each can be recognized as an authority. As such, they can legitimately use technical competence as a source of power to direct the efforts of workers so that the company's objectives can be accomplished. When organizations recognize an individual's technical credibility in the absence of technical competence, they are putting power in the hands of an incompetent person.

Ethical credibility.   Ethical credibility implies that a person is honest and sincere in dealings with people and agrees to be held accountable for all of his or her actions with them. In professional fields, practitioners subscribe to a code of ethics. The code represents a personal commitment that professional individuals will work to meet the needs of the people who have contracted for their products or services.

A code of ethics is structured to serve as a set of guidelines for professional conduct. The guiding principles specify behaviors that would be considered ethical and behaviors that would be unethical. Professional people are expected to devote their time and expertise in efforts to benefit the consumer client. The code prohibits professional people from meeting their own personal needs if doing so would jeopardize the consumer's opportunities for satisfaction. For example, if the professional person withheld, compromised, or misrepresented her expertise so that she could gratify her own personal needs, it would be a violation of ethical principles.

Probably the most famous of the ethical codes is the Hippocratic Oath. This basic rule of professional ethics was proclaimed by the Greek

physician Hippocrates over 2500 years ago: " . . . Above all, not knowingly to do harm." This oath stipulates that the professional person
promises not to intentionally harm anyone. What the oath does not
specifically address is what is meant by *intentionally*. If a patient dies
while under a doctor's care as a result of the normal course of a disease,
that care cannot be construed as having caused intentional harm. Suppose, however, that the family members openly questioned the doctor's
judgment and the doctor became defensive. Then, upon hearing the
conflict, the patient became agitated and subsequently died from complications of a coronary disease. Can the doctor's actions then be construed as intentionally causing harm? These kinds of issues are
discussed by professional committees on standards and ethics. They are
never easy to resolve.

In his book *Management*, Peter Drucker (1973) applied the concept
of ethical conduct to the work of a manager. Drucker made a rather
strong statement about the necessity for managers to make a personal
commitment to the professional ethic.

> There are important areas where managers, and especially busi-
> ness managers, still do not realize that in order to be permitted to
> remain autonomous and private they have to impose on them-
> selves the responsibility of the professional ethic. They still have to
> learn that it is their job to scrutinize their deeds, words, and
> behavior to make sure that they do not knowingly do harm.
>
>   . . . The manager who fails to think through and work for the
> appropriate solution to an impact of his business because it makes
> him "unpopular in the club" knowingly does harm. He knowingly
> abets a cancerous growth. That this is stupid has been said. That
> this always in the end hurts the business or the industry more than
> a little temporary "unpleasantness" would have hurt has been said
> too. But it is a gross violation of professional ethics.

Unlike physicians, people within business are not routinely
required to subscribe to a code of ethics. Nonetheless, society expects
them to behave just as though they had done so. It is regarded as simply
a matter of good business practice.

Professional people offer the benefits of their expertise to those
who seek their services. Making themselves available in this way says to
the public that this expertise will be given without prejudice or risk that
their judgments will be affected by special interests. They are obligated
to deliver their knowledge in a rational manner. This presumes that if
for any reason they are politically pressured or suffering from conditions
that prevent objective thinking (stress, fatigue, anger, pride, ambition,
greed, jealousy, and the like), they will not attempt to use their professional exterior to cover the demands stemming from their personal

needs. Otherwise, they would be in violation of the professional ethic; they would knowingly be doing harm. They would be placing their needs before the welfare of people who have entrusted their needs to their discretion.

If and when business people fail to scrutinize their actions, deeds, and words, as Drucker indicated, they are then in violation of a written or unwritten code of ethics. As such, they are then subject to the judgment of their own peers (whose job it is to uphold the ethical standards) as well as the opinions and perhaps even the laws of society.

Just as technical credibility is based on technical competence, ethical credibility is likewise based on a type of competence—namely, emotional stability. Unethical behavior in a business setting is related to the misuse of power. This misuse usually stems from impulses, emotional forces that trigger behavioral responses that occur without the guidance of thought or structured planning. The nature of such behaviors are generally self-protective, self-gratifying, and are often destructive to others. Although they can be considered as normal kinds of reactions in many situations, they are generally destructive to the welfare of an organization.

The job of people in authority is to use the company's power for the company's benefit, not for their own. The danger is, of course, that they may confuse, misconstrue, or even misrepresent their own needs as the company's needs. The result is an act of impulsive power solely for their own advantage that may be at the expense of some workers, the company, or both.

Unlike impulsive power, judicious power is under the constant control and scrutiny of a person's judgment. The power is based on making decisions through the process of reason, rather than purely on the basis of emotion. Prior to actually using power, the emotionally stable person weighs new information by fitting it into a network of preexisting information. Mistakes are kept to a minimum since many of them are anticipated in advance and thereby avoided. In the words of Levinson and Rosenthal (1984), the chief executive officers that they interviewed "had a powerful conscience, intellectual capacity and good judgment." These qualities, indeed, capture the essence of ethical credibility.

Interpersonal credibility. Interpersonal credibility is a third important factor in the consideration of establishing oneself as an authority within an organization. It is a basic human truth that force breeds contempt, resentment, and eventually rebellion. By contrast, the members of a work team who are directed by a person with interpersonal credibility have high levels of motivation and morale. The tension levels within the groups are relatively low and the levels of interworker support are usually quite high.

The core of interpersonal credibility lies within a person's ability to recognize and meet the needs of other people. Specific characteristics of interpersonal credibility typically include availability, approachability, patience, empathy, flexibility, consistency, tenderness, and honesty (Wilson, 1979). Workers under direction of such a person are generally loyal, competent, supportive, and happy. Much of an organization's success stems from the knowledge that the workers' contributions are vital to the organization's welfare. The ability to reflect that attitude throughout the organization at large, all the way down to one-on-one contact, is a direct reflection of an individual's interpersonal credibility.

Interpersonal credibility is the perception by a group of people that an individual understands and cares about what happens to them. They become convinced that this person recognizes their goals as important. People with interpersonal credibility use their powers to help group members reach their goals. The group members in turn recognize such people as authorities on the basis of their interpersonal credibility. They subsequently legitimize the authority's right to direct their efforts to meet objectives.

In summary, the concept of authority differs from that of power. Power is a force by which objectives can be accomplished. The organization's resources, human and otherwise are forms of power through which it can accomplish its objectives. The organization makes its powers available only to individuals that it recognizes as competent. An individual can become recognized as competent through technical, ethical, and interpersonal credibility. This recognition of competence results in the permission to use some range of the organizational powers and thus qualifies the individual as an authority within the organization.

In returning to the definitions of leadership and management, we can now apply each of the concepts we have discussed. As you will soon see, while leadership and management are interdependent, they are not identical functions.

Management

Management is specifically concerned with the direction of organizational resources. The manager's job essentially involves performing the tasks that were described under the section on "directive skills." To set task-related goals, to plan and problem solve, to facilitate work, to obtain and provide feedback, and to make control adjustments, the manager needs to have access to substantial amounts of the organization's power. The capacity to use this power is legitimized by the organization's recognition of the manager as an authority; that is, a person who is competent in specialty skills, directive skills, emotional stability, and interpersonal skills. The extent of the manager's authority is limited to specific areas or divisions within the organization over which the manager is charged with responsibility. While managers will very likely be expected to determine objectives for their particular divisions, they would not be very likely to perform decision-making functions that would influence the overall scope of the organization, nor would managers often be called upon to represent the organization outside their divisions or outside of the organization's immediate structural boundaries. To review, a manager is an individual who has the authority to direct specific organizational resources in order to accomplish objectives.

Leadership

A leader is an individual who has the authority to decide, direct, and represent the objectives and functions of an organization. From this definition, we can readily see that leadership incorporates the functions of management: namely, the direction of the organization's resources in order to accomplish objectives. Leadership goes beyond management in its other functions. A leader is responsible for the organization itself. As its chief representative, the leader is held accountable and responsible for the welfare and the actions of the organization. The organization, of course, can vary significantly in size, scope, and complexity. Regardless, the leader shapes the direction, manages the activities, and represents the policies and products as the person who has charge of the organization as a whole and integrated entity. The organization may be as small in size as a family, with one or both of the parents in the leadership role, or it may be a giant corporation with the chief executive officer "pulling the organization into the future" (Levinson and Rosenthal, 1984).

Some organizations may be led and managed by the same individual. For example, the owner and operator of a small business would very likely perform all of the leadership functions including the direction of the organization's resources. Other organizations employ leaders who may have developed a great deal of corporate wisdom as a manager before moving up the ladder to leadership.

Many of the skills needed for effective leadership stem from management. A good manager will likely have developed the knowledge and the skills for working with people. The effective leader will inevitably make use of these people skills. They will be needed when the leader makes decisions that will affect the people who serve the organization. They will also be needed when the leader represents the organization to the people it serves.

STRUCTURED TRAINING IN LEADERSHIP

Leadership training is certainly not a new concept. Many colleges with business programs offer courses pertaining to the principles of leadership. Beyond the college level, corporations themselves often hire consultants to teach leadership skills to their managers and supervisors. The problem of poorly prepared leaders cannot be explained then by the unavailability of leadership training. Instead, the problem relates more to the nature of the training.

Training for a position in leadership usually occurs in one of two types of settings: the college classroom and the business seminar. Each setting focuses its training models on different objectives.

Generally the college course concerns itself with an eclectic study that surveys the research fields of leadership theory. The professor's intent is to train the students to become critical and discriminating about the theoretical assumptions of the various points of view that are uncovered in the literature. Students quickly understand that there is no one best approach to becoming an effective leader. Success in leadership appears to depend upon a blend of personality characteristics among the leader and subordinates, the relationship between leadership behavior and situational variables, and the ways in which different forms of power can influence subordinate behavior (Yukl, 1981). The students are taught to view the sets of variables from these different approaches as being integrated in a meaningful way. Furthermore, they can learn that a great deal of progress has been made in identifying the determinants of effective leadership (Yukl, 1981). Unfortunately, definitive research is not yet available on the relationship between success in business school and actually becoming an effective leader.

Businesses have made their own attempts to train candidates for leadership through seminars. Compared to the college course, each seminar experience usually focuses the student's attention on one specific leadership training program. Such programs often include many simulated experiences designed to help the candidate apply the classroom principles to the challenges that they will face in the day-to-day responsibilities of actual leadership. Many mid- to large-size companies employ their own training personnel to directly teach or contract for training programs. Like college leadership courses, the actual value of leadership training through seminars is also unknown since the direct results are difficult to measure. Many university professors specializing in leadership express concern about this type of training. Participants often are unable to tell the difference between training methods that have been derived from scholarly research versus the approaches and claims made by trainers whose livelihood depends upon selling their own particular training program to a business.

If structured training is related to effective leadership, its success would very likely depend upon some mixture of theory and practice. This book focuses on one component of the theory-practice mix—namely, a leader's relationships with people. The purpose is to teach both the new and experienced leader important concepts that will illuminate some of the mysteries of people's actions and interactions. Despite its complexities, much of human behavior is logical and therefore predictable. Regardless of the leader's theoretical orientation and applied training, a solid grounding in "what makes people tick" will very likely enhance the capacities for effective leadership.

RATIONALE FOR PEOPLE STUDY IN LEADERSHIP

The humanistic psychologist Abraham Maslow (1954) wrote of the seven kinds of *needs* that influence human behavior. He arranged the needs in a hierarchy by order of importance: that is, the need for survival, security, love and belonging, self-esteem, self-actualization, knowledge, and order and balance. Maslow proposed that each successive need expressed itself only after the previous need had been at least partially satisfied.

Researchers and practitioners alike have attempted to apply the concept of Maslow's hierarchy to the relationship between leaders and their followers. In general, these applications focus on the notion that subordinates as well as leaders constantly struggle to satisfy their needs (Nierenberg, 1973).

Specific human behavior is a result of the individual's attempts to reduce the pressure of these needs. The leader can *influence* the behavior by providing channels through which the subordinate can satisfy the underlying needs. One reason then for studying the elements of human behavior in preparing for a position as a leader is to understand that the process of influencing subordinates is closely related to an appreciation for the factors that *motivate* subordinates.

McClelland (1975) applied the concept of motivation to self-confidence. He argued that the powers of force, charisma, and persuasive abilities cannot entirely explain the influence that leaders have over their subordinates. Instead, a leader's influence stems from the capacity to arouse confidence in the followers and to help them genuinely believe that they can accomplish the goals that they share.

Whatever the source of the leader's ideas, he cannot inspire his people unless he expresses vivid goals which in some sense they want. Of course, the more closely he meets their needs, the less "persuasive" he has to be; but in no case does it make sense to speak as if his role is to force submission. Rather it is to strengthen and uplift, to make people feel that they are the origins, not the pawns of the social system (deCharms, 1968). His message is not so much, "Do as I say because I am strong and know best. You are children with no wills of your own and must follow me because I know better," but rather, "Here are the goals which are true and right and which we share. Here is how we can reach them. You are strong and capable. You can accomplish these goals." His role is to make clear which are the goals the group should achieve, and then to create confidence in its members that they can achieve them.

Peters and Waterman (1982) reported that one of the factors that accounted for the success of many top-performing companies was the extent of control employees perceive they had over their own situations within the company.

He needs both to be part of something and to stick out. He needs at one and the same time to be a conforming member of a winning team and to be a star in his own right. . . . Men willingly shackle themselves to the nine-to-five if only the cause is perceived to be in some sense great. The company can actually provide the same resonance as does the exclusive club or honorary society. . . . So we observed time and again, extraordinary energy exerted above and beyond the call of duty when the worker (shop floor worker, sales assistant, desk clerk) is given even a modicum of apparent control over his or her destiny. . . . The mere knowledge that one can exert control made the difference.

IMPORTANT PEOPLE SKILLS OF TOP EXECUTIVES

Most experts currently agree that effectiveness in leadership is not directly associated with specific physical or personal traits. In other words, a leader with one set of traits might be effective in situation A, but be markedly less effective in situation B. For example, people who might have been leaders in their business classes might not necessarily succeed as leaders in the business world. Likewise, a successful military leader might have difficulty succeeding as an executive in a corporate setting. In addition, leaders with entirely different types of personalities might be equally effective in similar situations. Conceivably, the military leader and an ordained priest could each succeed as executives in a corporate setting.

Attempts to determine the components of leader effectiveness have shifted from the study of leadership traits to a focus on leadership skills. Research now concentrates more on the ways a person performs the responsibilities of leadership rather than on the nature of the leader's personality or physical characteristics. As cited in Yukl (1981), Stogdill summarized the actions associated with effective leadership:

> The leader is characterized by a strong drive for responsibility and task completion, vigor and persistence in pursuit of goals, venturesomeness and originality in problem solving, drive to exercise initiative in social situations, self-confidence and sense of personal identity, willingness to accept consequences of decision and action, readiness to absorb interpersonal stress, willingness to tolerate frustration and delay, ability to influence other persons' behavior, and capacity to structure social interaction systems to the purpose at hand.

In an attempt to determine how successful leaders of established organizations accomplished results, Levinson and Rosenthal (1984) interviewed chief executive officers from six major corporations. In their summary, they reported the following results about how these specific leaders related to people:

> Provided a vehicle for decision making that fostered consensus tempered by the willingness to make decisions where consensus was not achieved.
>
> Were ready to stimulate, implement and live with change.
>
> Were willing to take risks, make mistakes, learn from them, and afford subordinates the same opportunities.
>
> Relentlessly, but gently forced people to achieve clarity.
>
> Faced up to the pain and disappointment after firing, demoting, transferring and administering other forms of punishment for those who could not live up to standards.
>
> Developed support from others, learned how to use it, and how to offer that support in return.
>
> Could touch others in a personal way, warmly, consistently in such a manner that all could recognize his integrity.
>
> Insisted on exacting work to the extent that people needed to be prepared to defend their work.
>
> Were compassionate, empathic, sensitive to people's self-esteem and face-saving needs.
>
> Could put others at ease.

Attempted to obtain commitment rather than compliance by efforts to create an understanding of the problem.

Encouraged autonomy by offering support for collective decision making and extended permission to risk.

Used a mixture of pressure and praise to motivate.

Had great emotional control.

Could fuse their affection with their aggression.

Had the capacity for abstraction and the strength to take charge in order to pull the organization into the future.

Were straight with their people and trustworthy.

Were people growers.

McCall and Lombardo (1983) conducted a study in which they attempted to identify actions of executives that spelled the difference between success and failure. They found many similarities among twenty-one "derailed executives" and twenty "arrivers." In the words of McCall and Lombardo, "executives, like the rest of us, are a patch-work of strengths and weaknesses . . . there is no one best way to succeed." They described the derailed executives as "successful people who were expected to go even higher in the organization but who reached a plateau late in their careers, were fired, or were forced to retire early." They described the arrivers as "those who made it all the way to the top." Certain patterns emerged that the authors concluded could account for the differences between the two groups.

The fatal flaws of the derailers were summarized as follows:

Insensitive to others: abrasive, intimidating, bullying style.

Cold, aloof, arrogant.

Betrayal of trust.

Overly ambitious: thinking of next job, playing politics.

Specific performance problems with business.

Overmanaging: unable to delegate or build a team.

Unable to staff effectively.

Unable to think strategically.

Unable to adapt to a boss with a different style.

Overdependent on advocate or mentor.

Each derailed executive exhibited at least two of the fatal flaws. In fact, the arrivers sometimes had similar problems. In both groups, the flaws tended to emerge when one of five things happened to them:

1. They lost a boss who had covered or compensated for their weak-nesses.
2. They entered a job for which they were not prepared.

3. They left behind a trail of little problems or bruised people.
4. They moved up during an organizational shakeup and weren't scrutinized until the shake-down period.
5. They entered the executive suite, where getting along with others is critical.

The derailers handled the flaws in different ways than the arrivers. In general, their problems caught up with them as time went on and as they moved up in the organizational hierarchy. Company personnel described them in the following ways:

"moody or volatile under pressure"

"openly jealous of peers"

"frequent angry outbursts eroded the cooperation necessary for success"

"tended to react to failure by going on the defensive, trying to keep it under wraps while they fixed it"

The arrivers, on the other hand, knew how to work with people. The authors described the arrivers as individuals who would take the time and effort to understand other people's points of view. They were willing to change themselves and change their decisions. McCall and Lombardo stated, "That same flexibility, of course, is also what is needed to get along with all types of people." In contrast with the derailers' quick temper under pressure, the arrivers could generally remain calm. The arrivers were said to have handled their mistakes with poise and grace. Almost uniformly, they admitted their mistakes, forewarned others so that they would not be hurt by them, and then proceeded to correct them. They seldom blamed others, and once they dealt with the problems they did not dwell on them. The arrivers also had integrity:

Integrity seems to have a special meaning to executives. The word does not refer to simple honesty, but embodies a consistency and predictability built over time that says, "I will do exactly what I say I will do when I say I will do it. If I change my mind, I will tell you well in advance so you will not be harmed by my actions." Such a statement is partly a matter of ethics, but, even more, a question of vital practicality. This kind of integrity seems to be the core element in keeping a large, amorphous organization from collapsing in its own confusion.

A NECESSARY COMPONENT FOR EFFECTIVE LEADERSHIP

According to many experts, then, the effective leader has developed the knowledge, skills, and temperament for working with people. The actual traits of the leader's personality appear to be less important than the ways the leader actually treats the people who follow. The knowledge includes an understanding of factors that determine the "hows" and "whys" of typical human behavior in any number of situations. The skills involve knowing how to redirect human behavior from impulsive and self-serving actions into productive channels that can benefit both the worker as well as the organization. This temperament houses the capacity to base actions on forethought, purpose, and direction.

SUMMARY

The need to formally train people in leadership is becoming recognized as an economic necessity by American industry. The problem of poorly prepared leaders has been linked to the nature of the ways colleges and businesses have attempted to train leaders. Success in leadership appears to depend less on specific physical or personal traits than it does on the learning and application of specific leadership skills. This chapter has defined leadership and management and discussed the need for including the study of human behavior in any leadership training program.

Now, as we continue, the purpose of this book will be to acquaint the student of leadership with a concept of the knowledge, skills, and temperament necessary for effectively working with people. The book blends an operational framework for leadership with a dynamic theory of personality and a systems theory of human relationships. The theory of personality attempts to explain reasons why impulses sometimes interfere with sound judgment. The relationship theory describes how conflict can either disintegrate or strengthen the bonds between people. The procedural framework provides a model of leadership skills designed to redirect impulsive behavior into productive channels, use conflict to strengthen working relationships, and control the focus and direction of organizational activities.

TOPICS FOR DISCUSSION

1. What are the differences between leadership and management?

2. Relate some of the reasons why American industry has often been disappointed with the results of leadership training and then suggest alternatives that would be more likely to produce effective business leaders.
3. Discuss why an individual's physical and personal traits are less likely to be predictive of leadership effectiveness than an individual's training and experience.
4. What skills have been determined to play an important role in the development of leadership effectiveness?

RECOMMENDED READINGS

BLAKE, R. R., & MOUTON, J.S. (1981). *The versatile manager: A grid profile.* Homewood: IL: Irwin-Dorsey.

CHAPMAN, E. N. (1984). *Put more leadership into your style.* Chicago: Science Research.

FIEDLER, F. E., & CHEMERS, M. M. (1976). *Improving leadership effectiveness: The leader match concept.* New York: Wiley.

GOLDHABER, G. M. (1984). *Organizational communication* (3rd ed.) Dubuque, IA: Brown Company.

HERSEY, P., & BLANCHARD, K. (1982). *Management of organizational behavior* (4th ed.). Englewood Cliffs, NJ: Prentice-Hall.

LEVINSON, H., & ROSENTHAL, S. (1984). *CEO—Corporate leadership in America.* New York: Basic Books.

PETERS, T., & WATERMAN, R., JR. (1982). *In search of excellence.* New York: Harper & Row.

SAYLES, L. R. (1979). *Leadership: What effective managers really do . . . and how they do it.* New York: McGraw-Hill.

YUKL, G. A. (1981). *Leadership in organizations.* Englewood Cliffs, NJ: Prentice-Hall.

CHAPTER TWO
THE MECHANISMS
OF HUMAN BEHAVIOR

OUTLINE

MAJOR CONCEPTS
INTRODUCTION
THE RELATIONSHIP LIFE CYCLE
    Credibility
    Becoming Acquainted
    Forming Attachments
    Defining Expectations and Role Clarification
    Integration and Commitment
    Stability
    Jolts
    Instability
    Eroded Commitment
    Disintegration
    Adaptation to Change

THE BEHAVIOR OPERATING SYSTEM
    Homeostatic Programming
    The Dynamic Framework of Personality
    The Disruption of Rational Thinking
    A Case of Domestic Conflict
    An Analysis of the Case Study

SUMMARY
TOPICS FOR DISCUSSION
RECOMMENDED READINGS

MAJOR CONCEPTS

1. The Relationship Life Cycle is a model that illustrates how people develop a working relationship and either learn how to cope with their differences or face disintegration of that relationship because of conflicts they could not resolve.
2. The unsuccessful relationship follows a sequence of events marked by accumulating tensions from unresolved conflicts that end in the termination of the relationship.
3. The successful relationship follows a cycle through which conflicts are confronted and resolved so that the productive functions of the relationship are maintained.
4. The members of a relationship define their expectations and clarify the roles within the relationship through the channels of negotiation and from previous role models.
5. Through the direct route of negotiation, the proposed roles of each participant are put on the table for discussion, airing of differences, prospects for compromise, and ultimately for resolution.
6. *Modeling* determines the nature of the roles within the relationship based on the role models from the previous relationships of the participants.
7. Despite how erratic and irrational people sometimes might behave, their behavior follows logical principles.
8. As a human being, a leader is subject to a variety of strains, tensions, pressures, and even temptations, any of which can affect the capacity to reason, sense of judgment, and levels of patience. It is this human nature that can potentially divert the use of power from channels that would benefit the company into channels that would benefit the leader at the company's expense.
9. *Homeostasis* is the process by which the brain directs all of the cells, organs, and bodily systems to remain in a state of balance.
10. *Anxiety* is a signal to the brain that homeostasis is in danger.
11. The dynamic nature of human temperament is organized into three divisions of the personality.
12. The *id* is the emotional force that signals the brain to release behaviors that will relieve pain or discomfort.
13. The *superego* alerts the organism to the presence of potential danger by discharging feelings of anxiety.
14. The *ego* is the reasoning component of mental activity.
15. Without the necessary resources, the brain cannot support the normal operations of the ego. Subsequently, the superego floods the ego with anxiety, the ego shuts down, and the id orders an immediate discharge of impulsive activities in an attempt to relieve the threat to homeostasis.
16. The leader must get the ego operational before the tensions build

to a level where they have enough strike force to render it inoperative.

17. The leader must develop the technical and adaptive capacities of the ego. Then the ego can neutralize the anxieties of the superego and rechannel the urges from the id into ideas and thoughts that can be satisfied with reason and understanding.

INTRODUCTION

In Chapter 1 we learned that success in leadership is closely related to the notion of people skills. This chapter will provide you with insights about how people can be expected to function in working relationships. The principles will help you learn how to motivate people in your organization, anticipate problems that interfere with communication and cooperation, and redirect tensions into productive channels.

The chapter is divided into two main sections. The first section focuses on the working relationship. The concept you will be learning about is called The Relationship Life Cycle. Its purpose is to help you understand that even though conflict can destroy a relationship, it can also be the key to its growth. Working relationships follow a logical sequence in terms of how they begin, function, and in some cases stumble and disintegrate. As a leader, you can apply this concept to stabilize the working relationships in your organization. Research in leadership suggests that one of the strongest ways to motivate people is to support their self-esteem by making them an integral part of a problem-solving team (Yukl, 1981). The Relationship Life Cycle will help you understand how this theory actually works.

The second section of the chapter focuses on the idea that what goes on inside of people will ultimately determine whether their behavior will be guided by impulses or sound judgment. The concept that you will be learning about is called The Behavior Operating System. Its purpose is to help you understand that despite how erratic and irrational people sometimes act, their behavior follows logical principles. By discovering and integrating these principles, you will be better able to redirect impulsive behavior that could potentially harm the organization into productive channels that will support organizational goals.

THE RELATIONSHIP LIFE CYCLE

The Relationship Life Cycle is a theoretical model that represents how relationships develop, function, and in some cases disintegrate. The unsuccessful relationship follows a sequence of events marked by accumulating tensions over unresolved conflicts that end in the termination of the relationship. The successful relationship follows a cycle through which conflicts are confronted and resolved so that the productive functions of the relationship are maintained. The model applies to relationships in business as well as to social and family relationships.

The model consists of nine phases that will each be described in detail. To facilitate your understanding of the model, we will be looking at a case study, "The Owner Versus the Manager," as we proceed through the various steps of a working relationship.

Credibility

The first step within the model is called *credibility*. In this stage, the prospective members investigate the credentials of one another. The investigative process may take place formally or informally. A formal investigation might include reviewing resumes and professional testimonials. An informal investigation might include words of support from a mutual friend. Credibility is established when each of the prospective members believes that the other person can perform the functions expected within the relationship (see Fig. 2–1). The members likely have not met one another as yet. (If the mutual scrutiny is favorable to both parties, the relationship proceeds to the next step, which is called *becoming acquainted.)*

FIG. 2-1   The Relationship Life Cycle—Establishing Credibility

The Owner Versus the Manager

Barbara Collins is the owner of a video store. Her husband, Nathan, who established the business, recently died from a heart attack. Mrs. Collins knows very little about running a store, or about business practice in general. She placed an ad for a manager in a local trade journal. The person who responded was a man named John Baker. His credentials indicated that he currently managed a video store in a major shopping mall. Letters of reference documented that had it not been for Mr. Baker's expertise, the owners of the store would have been forced to go out of business. Instead, Mr. Baker had increased their profits significantly in less than one year. In his cover letter, he remarked that, although he was happy in his current position, the job description for Mrs. Collins' store fit very closely with his career objectives.

Becoming Acquainted

The second step is becoming acquainted. This process may include interviews, as might occur within a job setting, or informal conversations over coffee in a first-time social meeting. The nature of the interaction helps each person determine the other's qualifications for stepping into the roles of the potential relationship. The qualifications upon which the prospects measure one another involve how well each lives up to the other's expectations and personal desires. For example, the members of an audience might realize that a speaker's personal warmth is just as sincere as their master of ceremonies had led them to expect. As another example, a couple of college coeds might blissfully discover that they really do have as much in common as their matchmaking friends had promised. In either case, the individuals learn firsthand of the other's characteristics and qualifications. The relationship may terminate at this stage if either party is not satisfied. (See Fig. 2-2.)

FIG. 2-2 The Relationship Life Cycle—Becoming Acquainted

Mrs. Collins was impressed by the documents that Mr. Baker had forwarded. She decided that she would invite him for an interview. He arrived promptly, dressed appropriately, and expressed appreciation for the opportunity to learn more about the position. His conversation revealed that he knew a great deal about the video industry as well as about retail business. He acknowledged to Mrs. Collins that he would eventually like to develop a franchise of video stores that could operate at such volume that the price of movie rentals could be lower than any of the competition's.

From John's own point of view, Mrs. Collins badly needed help. She seemed to be a nice person who wanted to make her business succeed. He learned that her husband died shortly after he opened the store. His death left Mrs. Collins with a considerable financial obligation and virtually without resources to run the business. John sensed that she would give him a considerable amount of autonomy. Through his expertise and her support, they would make the business a great success.

Forming Attachments

In the next stage, the individuals form attachments to one another. Each has so far invested a certain degree of time and energy into the prospect of developing the relationship. As the process of becoming acquainted continues, each person begins to relax defensive guards and develops early forms of trust. In other words, they are who they say they are, they can do what they have said they can do, and they will not jeopardize the welfare of the other person in the relationship. Once this early trust begins to emerge, the individuals form an interconnective bond that represents the shell of the newly developing relationship. Each would feel at least some sense of regret and disappointment if the relationship would not develop beyond this point. (See Fig. 2–3.)

FIG. 2-3   The Relationship Life Cycle—Forming Attachments

Mrs. Collins began to get her hopes up that John would accept her offer for the position. She believed that he could run the store well. His self-confidence and authoritative manner gave her a sense of strength that made her feel that the business could succeed. He seemed to know what he was talking about, had great visions for what the store could accomplish, and had the courage to make it all work. She worried though that he might not feel challenged enough in such a small-time operation.

John hoped he hadn't come on too strong. This lady seemed anxious anyway. The last thing she needed was some high-pressure type person to shake up what little self-confidence she had. He really did want the position. By building it to its economic potential, he could make a great deal of money and, perhaps, eventually move into a partnership.

Defining Expectations and Role Clarification

Following the attachment stage, the individuals take an active role in developing the relationship by formulating the functions of each member. An effective leader will specify the tasks that he expects the subordinate to perform. The subordinate will indicate the extent of his willingness and ability to comply with these expectations. Negotiations may occur, limitations will be defined, and consequences for hard work, success, and failure will be delineated.

The participants in this phase of the relationship life cycle will define their expectations and clarify relationship roles through two possible channels. One channel is through direct negotiations, and the other is through a process called modeling. Through the direct route of negotiation, the roles that each participant would like to perform as well as have the other person perform are put on the table for discussion, airing of differences, prospects for compromise, and ultimately for resolution. They might begin their discussion based on the roles as defined by the job description. The subordinate might state reasons for wanting to change certain aspects of the proposed position such as working hours, benefits, and compensation. After considering the subordinate's needs and wishes, the leader might adapt his or her expectations and modify the proposed roles in ways that might work for both parties.

The process of defining expectations and clarifying roles could also occur through modeling. *Modeling* determines roles within the relationship through an unconscious process based on role models from the person's previous relationships. That is, the participants "carve out" their respective roles in ways through which they may be totally unaware. The structure of people's lives are often determined from past influences. Adult relationships frequently resemble relationships that shaped a child's life. For example, a male subordinate might expect that a female boss will behave toward him in ways that are similar to the way his mother related to him as a child. The female boss might behave toward a male subordinate either in a manner similar to the way her mother related to her father or to the ways she herself related to her younger brothers. The female subordinate might expect her male boss to relate to her in a manner similar to the way her father treated her mother, to the way her father treated her, or to the way she was treated by her older brothers.

To illustrate how past models really do affect one's current relationships, consider who performs certain roles within your own family today. For example, who washes the clothes versus who mows the lawn? Who makes arrangements for the babysitter versus who pays the check in a restaurant? Now consider the family you grew up in. Are the roles that you currently perform as a husband or wife more similar to those that your mother performed or to those that your father performed? If what you are doing now is in any way similar to the things your parents did when you were a child, then the roles that characterize your current relationship have probably been influenced by the process of modeling.

Modeling is no more or less effective a means for determining roles within a relationship than is negotiation, as long as it works. When it does not, you can make your expectations much more clear to the other person by expressing them openly through the process of negotiation. As a result, both of you have a better chance of finding out what you want for yourselves and from the other person. (See Fig. 2–4.)

FIG. 2-4   The Relationship Life Cycle—Clarifying Roles

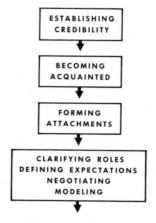

Both Mrs. Collins and John Baker felt optimistic about the prospects for their working relationship. Mrs. Collins stated very clearly that John would have freedom to make decisions regarding matters that concerned the day-to-day operations in the store. She expected him to consult with her prior to altering any of the existing store policies.

John indicated his willingness to work in line with her expectations. However, he did not feel that he could accept the position at the salary that she offered him. With his knowledge of the video industry and his realistic potential for increasing the store's profits, he believed that he should have more money. He clearly stated the dollar figure he needed in order to become the store manager.

Mrs. Collins considered his comments for a long time. However, she said that she could not meet the figure. After a great deal of discussion, they developed a plan through which John could share any profits that would exceed the store's current level of net receipts.

Mrs. Collins felt tremendous relief when John said he would accept the position. She was certain that the prospects for paying off her business loan were no longer in question. John was someone that she could count on to make the business run the way Nathan had developed it. Afterall, he had intended it to be a neighborhood store. Their customers were their friends and neighbors. New customers had come in by word of mouth. Nathan loved to cater to them. She sensed that this warmth toward people was just as important to John.

As for John, the position was ideal. He would finally have his own store to run the way he saw fit; no more having to answer to some corporation that ran the operation from across the country. He knew he could bring Mrs. Collins around to the latest trends in the industry. It might take time, but he had a way with people like her.

Integration and Commitment

Once the roles have been clarified and mutually understood, the individuals strengthen their attachment to one another, forming what becomes a sense of integration and commitment. They begin to regard one another as members of a functioning unit. They develop camaraderie and loyalty to one another as well as to the organization itself. People outside of the unit recognize the relationship as a separate and viable entity. (See Fig. 2–5.)

Mrs. Collins held a grand opening sale to introduce the community to her new manager. She walked John up to people arm in arm and talked about how Nathan would have been so proud to have him on board.

John praised the wisdom of the Collins' family for their service to the community. He greeted the customers on behalf of the store and talked to them about the movies they would like the store to carry.

FIG. 2-5   The Relationship Life Cycle—Commitment

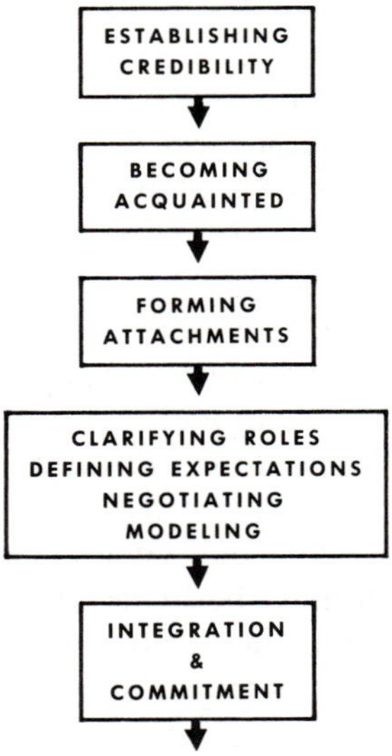

```
┌─────────────────┐
│  ESTABLISHING   │
│   CREDIBILITY   │
└─────────────────┘
         ↓
┌─────────────────┐
│    BECOMING     │
│   ACQUAINTED    │
└─────────────────┘
         ↓
┌─────────────────┐
│     FORMING     │
│   ATTACHMENTS   │
└─────────────────┘
         ↓
┌───────────────────────┐
│   CLARIFYING ROLES    │
│ DEFINING EXPECTATIONS │
│     NEGOTIATING       │
│      MODELING         │
└───────────────────────┘
         ↓
┌─────────────────┐
│   INTEGRATION   │
│        &        │
│   COMMITMENT    │
└─────────────────┘
         ↓
```

Stability

As the individuals begin performing the roles, the relationship becomes operational, serving the purpose of fulfilling the collective and individual needs of its members. In a business setting, the relationship accomplishes the company's objectives. In a social setting, the relationship takes care of interpersonal needs. As the needs and objectives are met through the functions carried out by the members, the relationship enters a period of stability. It runs smoothly and does what the individual members expect it to do. Each member performs the functions in accordance with the other's expectations, and neither behaves in a surprising or disturbing manner. (See Figure 2–6.)

Throughout the first quarter of John's role as the store's manager, the amount of business began to grow noticeably. With Mrs. Collins' approval, he implemented a system for checking out the video tapes by computer. Customers were thrilled when they could reserve the "hottest" titles at times to suit their schedule. They knew they could count on the movies being there in the store when they came to call for them.

Mrs. Collins was available to consult with John on a regular basis. His watchful eye of the industry trends and his sense of responsibility to the business enabled her to have a life of her

FIG. 2-6   The Relationship Life Cycle—Stability

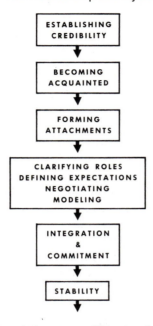

own again outside of the store. She simply didn't need to be there day and night anymore. Not only was she drawing a nice salary, but she began to prepay on her loan and even started to make long-term investments.

Jolts

At some point, an obstacle will arise that interferes with the operations of the relationship. One of the members behaves in a manner that disturbs the other. The behavior is inconsistent with the other's expectations. This disturbance is called a "jolt." Jolts can and do occur in the most functional of relationships. By themselves, jolts simply reflect that one person's needs are never completely understood by another, nor do they ever remain constant. As such, changes that emerge in the role performance of one person may cause tension within the other person and disrupt the stability of the relationship. (See Fig. 2–7.)

Tuesday was Mrs. Collins' customary day for checking the mail and paying bills. John had been out to lunch when she came in. After greeting the counter attendant, she went into her office

FIG. 2-7   The Relationship Life Cycle—The Jolt

and closed the door. She liked to hear the sound of business from the intercom Nathan had installed, so she turned it on and then proceeded to deal with her mail.

A few minutes later, John came back into the store. Mrs. Collins was somewhat surprised when she heard him raise his voice to the employee who had been attending the counter.

"Get off your rear end," John said in a condescending voice. "Don't just sit around when their aren't any customers."

"What am I supposed to do?" the employee asked meekly. "It was always okay with Nathan for me to watch a movie when I was waiting for a customer."

"Don't you ever let me hear you call him Nathan again," John said in a scolding tone of voice. "You refer to him as Mr. Collins and to his wife as Mrs. Collins. Get it in your head that I'm your boss now. You are not to be watching movies at any time unless a customer wants to see a portion of one before renting it. As far as what you're supposed to do, restock the movies, sweep the floor, and dust the counters. Don't be sitting around."

Mrs. Collins had never heard John talk to anyone like that before. She couldn't believe it. He left again for an appointment before she had a chance to say anything to him. Besides, she was so taken aback by it all, she wasn't sure what she would have said.

Instability

During this period of instability, the relationship no longer functions smoothly. The interactions between the individuals become strained, and their functions may be performed inefficiently or perhaps even at the expense of the other person. At this point the relationship does not run smoothly, nor does it serve the needs in the manner each of the individuals would like it to.

Unfortunately, it is difficult for many people to talk about their differences; especially when such differences cause problems in the relationship. It is often easier to try to overlook a problem or to perhaps find a "bandaid" solution. The intent is to get the relationship back on a stable course again. When the attempted solutions bypass or cover up the jolt, however, seeds are sewn for festering tension. In domestic situations, couples commonly deal with marital problems by taking vacations, moving to another house, changing jobs, or perhaps by even having a baby. None of these attempts really do anything about the differences that are growing between them. In business relationships, people sometimes express their anger and frustration by making sarcastic remarks or by talking behind the other person's back. These maneuvers sometimes help the angered person to calm down enough to get back into a facade of stability in the working relationship. Since the jolt itself was never actually resolved, the tension between the two members lies just under the surface waiting to erupt at the first sign of the next conflict. (See Fig.2–8.)

About a week had gone by since Mrs. Collins heard John scolding the employee. She had been in the store several times since then, but found herself avoiding John. She felt almost as though he had scolded her. She kept meaning to say something to him, but she never found the right moment.

One day while she was sitting at her kitchen table, she got a call from one of the customers, a Mrs. Filmore. The person told her that John had treated her very rudely. He upset her so much that she was considering not coming back.

"What happened?" Mrs. Collins asked with great concern.

"Well, I know you have this policy about charging fifty cents if

FIG. 2-8   The Relationship Life Cycle—Instability

the movies aren't returned by 7 o'clock in the evening. Last night, my basement leaked and I couldn't get over to the store in time. Well, little Freddy, the boy behind the counter wasn't going to charge me the fifty cents. Then, Mr. Baker found out about it. I told him what happened and that Nathan never would have charged me."

"What did Mr. Baker say?" Mrs. Collins asked. "He said that Nathan almost ruined this business and that if I wanted to keep my membership in the store's video club, I would pay the money. Then he grabbed the movie out of my hands. He grabbed it! I said to him, 'We'll just see about this, young man.' Then I walked out."

"Mrs. Filmore, I am so sorry that happened. I'm sure that Mr. Baker must not have been feeling well. Please accept my apologies. I would personally like to give you your next ten movie rentals without charging you."

"Oh, that won't be necessary, dear. I feel better just talking about it. I tell you, though, I won't go back in the store when that Mr. Baker is there," the woman said.

Mrs. Collins decided to say something to John this time. She made a trip into the store that next day and told him to come into her office right away.

"John," she started, "Mrs. Filmore called me last night and told me how rudely you treated her. I want to hear what you have to say about it."

"Mrs. Collins, don't come in here all of a sudden and start playing boss with me after five months," John said defensively. "You have no reason to complain. Your profits are up and so is your free time. If I'm going to make this store work for you, you have got to give me a free hand. Maybe I came on a little strong. I'm sorry. But you can't watch over every little thing I do".

Something about the way John talked to her was making her feel more like the employee than the boss. "What am I supposed to do when I get a call from customers who are upset because of the way you treated them?" she asked.

"Mrs. Collins, no store can please all of the people who walk into it. You do your best with most everyone. Our balance sheet from last quarter is proof enough. Let me worry about the customers, okay?" he asked reassuringly. "Don't worry, please."

"He did make me feel better," Mrs. Collins thought. "Besides, Mrs. Filmore was unreasonable herself sometimes." The next time she was in the store to do her office work, she would make a point of calling Mrs. Filmore to give her the free movies.

During the next two weeks, more and more customers called Mrs. Collins with complaints about John. Two of the counter attendants quit, and others were keeping to themselves when they worked.

Eroded Commitment

If the partners in a relationship do not resolve jolts as they occur, tension mounts and intensifies over time. More and more jolts crop up. The commitment and integration that once bound the partners together begins to erode. Their working relationship becomes marred by resentment, mistrust, and emotional distance. One partner starts to believe rumors about the other person and wonders how to defend him- or herself against what the other person might do. Necessity or convenience rather than camaraderie now keeps the physical structure of the relationship intact. (See Fig. 2–9.)

FIG. 2-9   The Relationship Life Cycle—Eroded Commitment

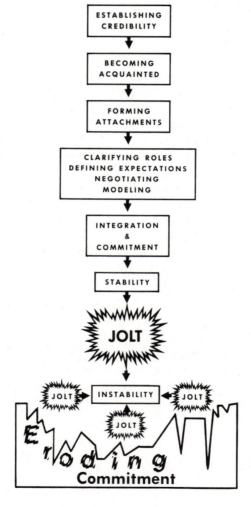

Mrs. Collins came into the store once again for her Tuesday office work. She started sorting the mail when, about half way down the pile, she noticed a business envelope from a supplier that she didn't recognize. The return address read "Adult

Capers, Inc." She examined the invoice and discovered that John had ordered several thousand dollars in pornographic titles. The company promised delivery by the fifteenth of the month. That was tomorrow.

She was shocked and felt betrayed. Her skin was flushed and her heart pounded relentlessly. Nathan always insisted that adult titles would never have a place in the store. He condemned other dealers for making such trash available. Now, all of a sudden this bill appears on her desk. She struggled with all sorts of feelings. Not only was she upset about this filth John ordered, but he had been causing bad will with many of the store's long-time customers. She wondered what happened to the commitment he had given her about clearing new policies with her first. She didn't know what to do. He was bringing more money in the store than she ever thought possible. But he was doing it in a way that she could never support. He went behind her back, he had been alienating the customers, and he had berated the employees. As far as she was concerned, he was hurting the store more than helping it. She decided that she would have to let him go.

Disintegration

When relationships do not mold to fit the changing needs of their members, additional jolts occur and eventually the commitment begins to erode. Continued erosion of the commitment spawns additional jolts, and eventually the members disintegrate. The relationship often terminates, usually with a great deal of resentment and hostility. (See Fig. 2–10.)

Adaptation to Change

Conflict between people is completely normal. It is a natural way through which individual differences are expressed. People never stay the same. As such, their needs for their life also change. In order for a working relationship to remain functional, it has to accommodate the changes that its members experience. Conflict arises between the members when they change in ways that threaten one another. One member perceives that the other member may be trying to hurt them in some way. This perception triggers anxiety. The natural reaction is to try to defend oneself against what feels like an attack. Often the defense takes

FIG. 2-10   The Relationship Life Cycle—Disintegration

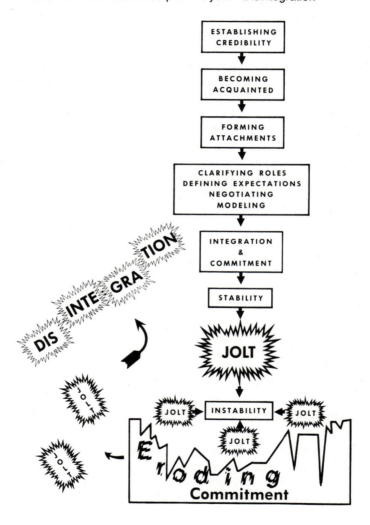

the form of a counterattack. The stage is then set to intensify the conflict rather than to see it resolved.

The most effective way to deal with a jolt is to recycle the conflict back to the phase of role clarification. By recognizing that the strained interaction actually represents some need that the relationship is not meeting, both individuals have an opportunity to renegotiate their roles within the relationship. In other words as one or both of them change— or perhaps their life outside the relationship changes in some unexpected way—they can work together so that the relationship can expand to accommodate the change (see Fig. 2–11). This process would involve identifying their differences, discussing their individual needs, and negotiating ways to accommodate one another.

The relationship life cycle is a model that illustrates how people develop working relationships and either learn how to cope with their differences or face disintegration of that relationship because of conflicts they could not resolve. An important concept for a leader to understand

FIG. 2-11   The Relationship Life Cycle—Adapting To Change

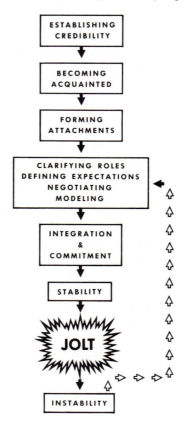

is that despite how erratic and irrational people sometimes act, their behavior follows logical principles. The purpose of this section is to describe how human temperament affects the nature of power in leadership.

THE BEHAVIOR OPERATING SYSTEM

Power is a vital tool for leadership to be effective. Without power, the leader will be incapable of directing human resources. The leader obtains power through recognition as an authority. Technical credibility provides access to the powers of the employing institution. Ethical credibility permits the use of power on behalf of society. Interpersonal credibility legitimizes the rights to control the efforts of fellow human beings.

The ultimate purpose of power in leadership is to accomplish objectives. The objectives for most businesses specifically relate to making a profit and delivering a service. The leader's own personal needs are of secondary importance. However, the distinction between the needs of the business versus the needs of the leader can at times become somewhat less than clear.

A leader's use of power is almost always entirely dependent upon human nature. Unlike the consistency of a finely tuned instrument, a leader's ability to use power often changes, sometimes drastically from one minute to the next. In some situations, leaders remain calm, level headed, and after careful judgment they make rational decisions. At other times, they are irritable, impatient, overly sensitive and, as a result, decisions are made impulsively. As a human being, a leader is subject to a variety of strains, tensions, pressures, and even temptations, any of which can affect the capacity to reason, the sense of judgment, and levels of patience. It is this human nature that can potentially divert the use of power from channels that would benefit the company into channels that would benefit the leader at the company's expense.

The purpose of this section is to describe how human temperament affects the nature of power in leadership. The operation of the human nervous system is governed by a series of inherently logical principles. The leader who develops an understanding of these principles can learn to rechannel impulsive energies into productive channels so that personal needs can be satisfied by supporting rather than jeopardizing the company, its workers, and its clientele.

Homeostatic Programming

The notion that power can be impulsively determined suggests that it is sporadic, unpredictable, and nonsystematic. On the contrary, impulsive power operates on a type of guidance system that is methodical, structured, and goal directed. What it lacks is conscious premeditation.

The brain generates powerful and pressuring emotions as the means by which it manages threats to bodily functions. The language of the human brain has often been compared to a kind of computer program. A program provides the instructions that define which functions the computer will perform. The brain is composed of many different systems, each of which performs its own specific set of functions. Despite the uniqueness of each of these systems, the thread that unites their operations is the program that keeps the body alive;—the will to survive. The brain integrates the components of this program through a concept known as homeostasis.

The Dynamic Framework of Personality

Homeostasis is the process by which the brain directs all of the cells, organs, and bodily functions to remain in a state of balance. The process, directed by billions of neurochemical interactions, is housed within twelve billion nerve cells and travels along fifteen quadrillion of the brain's circuits. In many ways, the field of neurochemical research represents the next frontier as it largely remains a mystery to scientific understanding. Despite their anatomical secrets, the operations of the brain unfold quite clearly when viewed from the perspective of personality. The dynamic nature of personality is organized into three divisions: the ego, the id, and the superego.

The ego is part of the personality that is organized to think. Thinking is a process by which a person takes in a set of information through the sense organs, compares that information to previously stored information, draws similarities and differences, categorizes it, and uses that information as a basis for making decisions. The ego thus analyzes situations from a wide variety of perspectives, determines the most appropriate solutions to a problem, anticipates complications that might result, develops contingency plans, and then carefully implements decisions (Hall, 1954). In many cases, the process becomes automated so that habits can be formed to reduce the energy needed for performing repetitive behaviors. The complexities of the ego and its functions far exceed the capabilities of even the most advanced computers. To match the abilities of the human brain, a computer would need to be ten thousand times its size (Newsweek, 1983).

The question then arises as to why people have difficulty solving all of their problems. If the ego is indeed so capable and efficient, why do we as people experience frustration and unhappiness? It has often been said that people use only a fraction of their brain's potential. One neurologist even claims that the computing potential of today's micro-computers could easily be matched by only *one* of the brain's 12 billion nerve cells (Newsweek, 1983). Once again, with all of this neurological potential, wherein lies the source of the ego's limitations as a problem solver? The answer, at least in part, becomes apparent by considering the two other dimensions of the personality; the id and the superego.

The id, like the ego, is also a problem solver. However, its approach to solving problems is very much different from that of the ego. Instead of thinking things through in a patient, objective, and rational manner, the id reacts impulsively to problems in one of two ways. It will either order actions to escape from a source of pain through some sort of avoidance or withdrawal or it will order actions designed to forcefully remove the source of pain.

The *id* is the emotional force that signals the brain to "okay" actions that will bring about immediate relief to pain. This pain can be in any form. It may be the ache from which a baby suffers when its stomach is empty, or it can be the anger brewing in an adult after a reprimand from a boss. The id tries to produce some type of immediate, crisis-oriented response in order to ease the pain.

The id is totally self-centered. It can only regard another person as either a provider or a competitor. The reason that it exists is to insure survival through immediate action. Its only concern is to provide an immediate solution that will take away the pain and/or to provide a source of pleasure. If it regards another person as a provider, it will pressure the brain into ordering actions designed to endear the provider into providing more. If it regards another person as a competitor—that is, someone who threatens to take away pleasure or to render pain—it will call for actions intended to eliminate that threat.

Positioned at the controls of a "helpless" infant's body, the id dutifully insures that the child's biological functions will be satisfied without delay, e.g., "The baby cries to be fed." But what would happen if the id were positioned at the controls of a six foot seven inch, two hundred eighty pound man who was following a young coed walking back to her dorm after an evening class? Remember, the id is totally self-centered and aims to satisfy the biological needs of the body by either removing the source of pain or by finding a source of pleasure. As far as the id is concerned, there is no regard for the welfare of any object outside of the body. The id would signal the brain to order the same actions whether it was inside of a three-month-old or a thirty-year-old body. Since it is programmed for self-satisfaction and ultimately concerned with biological preservation, it *never* grows up. It is constantly functioning, seldom sleeps, never changes, and always "lives" for the moment.

Impulses stem from the id. When you yell an obscenity at another driver, slam your fist on a desk out of frustration, stuff yourself to the point of pain at a restaurant, charge purchases you cannot actually afford, scream at your children beyond reasonable limits, you are responding out of your id. Just as an infant feels stomach pains and cries in an attempt to stop the hurt, so an adult similarly acts impulsively in attempting to get relief from some other kind of hurt. These adult hurts might take the form of frustration, humiliation, fear, anxiety, jealousy, loneliness, depression, tension, stress, and the like. No matter what form they take, each of these emotions becomes equated with sensations of pain. Since the id never grows up, it reacts to this pain in the same way it did when the body was in its infancy. The id always perceives pain as a serious threat to the body's safety.

In other words, regardless of the body's age, the id is that part of the personality that functions to keep the body alive. It is the component of the human being that is most like the animal's instinct to survive. It serves as the catalyst for satisfying all of the body's needs to consume, to eliminate, to stay warm, to protect itself and, overall, to stay alive. It will attempt to destroy anything that interferes by whatever means it can. It knows no limits, has no boundaries, and follows no external rules. It is governed totally by the principles of (1) eliminating pain and (2) providing pleasure. As one of the three components of the personality, it serves a vital role in the process of homeostasis.

If both the ego and the id serve as problem solvers, just what determines which will be used by the personality at any given time? What seems obvious, of course, is that the ego will solve problems when the body is in no apparent danger and can afford the luxury to think rather than to flee or fight. The id will solve problems by some sort of survival tactic when the body is faced with some life threatening circumstance. While this arrangement is generally true, it does not always account for our problem solving methods. For example, why might a boss ridicule a subordinate in front of his peers, a situation that results in a great deal of shame and embarrassment? Was such an action on the part of the boss the ego's solution to a problem or a solution by the id? If the action was driven by impulsive behavior, the boss's ego was shut down and the id was in control. Why did the ego shut down? Why didn't the boss handle the situation with better judgment? Certainly, the boss wasn't faced with any life endangering situations. There was no physical necessity to call in the "big guns." The answer to these questions will become clear by considering the third component of the personality, the superego.

The superego is that part of the personality that floods the ego with fear and anxiety. Fear is the emotion that signals an immediate danger or loss. Anxiety signals that a danger or loss is very likely to occur in the near future. The purpose of the superego is to provide signals to the ego that homeostasis is in danger. The effect of those signals is the perception by the ego that it is in pain. The superego responds with great speed to whatever sensory information it perceives as potentially threatening. The perceived danger could be as extreme as an oncoming vehicle that is about to broadside your car. It could be, however and often is, much less extreme. For example, if your boss were to say something like, "I don't need any of your wiseoff comments to the customer when I'm about to close the sale," you could become *superego triggered*. What that means is that your boss's comment hit you in a vulnerable spot. Your superego internalized this comment, transformed it into anxiety, and channeled that anxiety into your ego. Your ego then felt pain. At this point, you now have a problem. Will the problem be managed by your ego or will the problem be handled by your id? We will address this question shortly. For now, consider that the superego's function is to make you aware that homeostasis is threatened. It does so by using a form of communication that you will readily understand; namely, it puts you in pain. If your ego deals with the pain directly, you will react to the problem rationally, patiently, and objectively; in other words, with good sense. If, however, your ego does not cope with the problem and fails to get rid of the pain, the pain will remain in your system. Recall that the id's job is to get rid of the pain in its own specialized way; either by ordering actions that will get you far away from it or by ordering actions to forcefully destroy whatever is causing it.

The Disruption of Rational Thinking

The question arises as to why the ego does not manage the anxiety. What happens to the power of reason and judgment as resources to cope with life's difficulties? As a type of living computer, the brain requires sources of fuel in order to operate efficiently. When supplies of fuel run low, many of the operations the brain uses for thinking cease to run smoothly.

Medical research has confirmed that alterations in the brain's chemistry can affect behavior. Dr. Lendon Smith, a pediatrician, is the author of several books on the relationship between brain chemistry and inappropriate behavior (Smith, 1976).

Smith described a young child of perhaps 7 years. The child took some candy from a local supermarket. Why? According to Smith, the boy had eaten breakfast three to four hours earlier that was loaded with table sugars (donuts, cereal, jam, etc). After enjoying a brief though intense surge of energy, the boy began suffering a type of sugar withdrawal attack once the brain finished utilizing the sugars from his breakfast. Without sufficient sugar reserves that are derived from other food groups, the brain began to operate inefficiently. The child became tired, agitated, irritable, and hungry. Reacting out of biological desperation, his impulses drove him to seek additional doses of sugar. Perhaps even without conscious awareness, he then took the candy. Smith stated that the boy would probably not even remember having done so.

As a physician, Smith claims that a person's physical and emotional states are directly determined by the chemical balance in the brain. While the exact relationships have not been determined by medical science, Smith strongly argues that alterations in blood sugars can cause people to feel tense and irritable. He also raised the possibility that the very presence of stress and tension can themselves cause the brain to use higher than normal levels of sugars. The result would be inefficient operations within the brain which would likely interfere with clear thinking and subsequently trigger impulsive behaviors.

Interference with the normal activities of the brain can block the normal operations of the ego. In other words, the ego can be effectively shut off by altering the brain's blood chemistry. Smith's arguments strongly suggest that stress in the form of tension, pressure, and frustration consume the brain's nutrients at a tremendous rate, thus effectively lowering the levels to a degree that interferes with the process of rational thinking.

Anxiety is a signal to the brain that homeostasis is in danger. Presuming that the brain has adequate fuels already, it will more than likely manage the anxiety through reason and judgment. However, if fuel is in short supply the operations of the brain may not be able to withstand the stress, and they will ultimately collapse. At that point the brain's thermostat registers danger and opens the circuits to impulsive behavior. In other words, the ego functions adequately as long as it is properly maintained. If the superego floods it with anxiety, a healthy and efficient ego will either bury the anxiety in storehouses of forgotten memories (repression) or it will neutralize the anxiety through the rational process of problem solving. By contrast, the unstable and inefficient ego will lose its reasoning and judgment capabilities when flooded with anxiety by the superego. The id then comes on line in attempt to remove the sources of pain that are threatening to destabilize homeostasis.

Without the necessary levels of fuel (blood sugars and neurochemical transmitters), the brain simply cannot support the operations of ego. However, if the id and superego deplete the ego's fuel supplies before it can displace or remove the anxiety, the ego's operations will cease. Rational thinking will give way to urges and impulses.

When the superego does flood the ego with anxiety, the id recognizes the anxiety as a form of pain. Recall that the primary function of the id is to remove threats to homeostasis. Consequently, if the ego cannot remove the anxiety through its means of rational thinking or through repression, the id will remove it through impulse gratification—usually through aggressive behavior.

It is interesting to consider that what Smith has described from a biochemical point of view in the 1980s, Freud began describing from a psychological perspective in the 1890s. Freud said that the ego had no energy of its own. The first order of business it always survival. Survival is the id's primary concern (Hall, 1954). The id is the body's emotional link with its internal needs. Remember, the body signals the brain about its needs by making it sense pain. The body's energy from its fuel supplies are first delivered to the id. When the id has no pressing needs to fill, then remaining energies are routed to the ego. However, when the id "believes" that the body is in some state of deprivation, it diverts energies from the ego back for its own use. As this rechanneling of energies occurs, the person will likely shift from actions that have been planned through organized thinking to thoughtless actions that are determined almost exclusively on the basis of impulse (Hall, 1954).

We have seen from both a biochemical and a psychological perspective that the ego's ability to solve problems through rational thinking can be impaired by stress and tension. Abnormal levels of blood chemistry can bring on the stress and tension. And in turn, stress and tension can further lower the brain's levels of blood chemistry. It is a vicious cycle.

For the ego to function as a problem solver, two conditions must be satisfied. First, the ego must be in good working order. When it is not, the id takes over and influences the body to perform actions impulsively. Second, the ego must have access to all relevant information. To solve a problem on a rational basis, it must be able to consider a variety of options and choose the one that will best satisfy the needs of the situation. Given access to this information, the ego would be well equipped to solve problems. Without such access the ego would become virtually nonoperational. Even if it is functioning at full capacity with regard to healthy brain metabolism, the ego cannot do its job unless it is well informed.

In other words, if we can get information into the ego, it can do the job for which it is best equipped: solve problems by rational thinking. If information is prevented from reaching the ego, our problems will be dealt with on the basis of emotions, impulsive reactions, and aggressive behavior.

The following case study of a domestic conflict will illustrate how two individuals resort to impulsive power as a means by which each maintains their own internal stability. The analysis that follows the case study will consider how the three parts of the personality in each individual reacted and counterreacted in attempting to preserve internal homeostasis at the other person's expense. It is essential for leaders to recognize when they are being gripped by emotions and to know how these emotions affect behavior. This basic awareness is itself a function of the ego. By recognizing the presence of these emotional conditions, the leader will be making a transition from the id and superego into a state of consciously controlling the actions through the ego.

A Case of Domestic Conflict

Kathy Robins recently passed her state law boards and joined a large law practice. She developed her own caseload and won several disputes both in and out of court on behalf of her clients. Kathy thrived on her work, but deeply felt that her husband would always come first in her life. Today, she and Mike have been married for one year. As early as three weeks ago, she began rearranging her schedule so that she could devote the entire day to preparing for celebrating with Mike.

Kathy spent most of the morning at the market buying all of the things that would make the feast that she and Mike deserved. Dinner would begin at 6 o'clock with Caeser salad by candlelight. Kathy would then serve Chateaubriand with Japanese vegetables. Red wine would compliment the entire evening, with enough in reserve to toast their happiness for the next seventy-five years.

After scrubbing the house down to a sparkle during most of the afternoon, Kathy began preparing dinner around 4 o'clock. She left word at the office to have Mike call at home since he usually tried to call her at least once a day; but as yet, he hadn't done so. She set the table with their white linen tablecloth, china, silver, and their lead crystal stemware. As she finished the table, she admired how pretty it all looked and was proud that she and Mike would soon be sharing it. For a fleeting moment, she felt a pang of disappointment that Mike's applications to medical school had been rejected, and she also regretted that she had pressured him so much to give up the field of professional sales.

Sometimes she wondered if she really was much different from her mother. She didn't think she was nearly as critical or as judgmental. She hoped that she didn't belittle Mike the way her mother did with her father. No matter what Kathy's father did, it never seemed to be good enough; her mother always found something wrong with what he said, how he looked. The pathetic part about it was that her father had put up with it for all these years. Of course, her mother treated Kathy the same way. "Why would any girl want to become a lawyer? You can't keep a house and home together and please a husband and have a career too, dear," she would always say. "And why Mike, Kathy honey?" her Mom would warn her. "Mike will never amount to anything. He's too wild. He'll flit between one job and another, and mark my words, someday you'll catch him playing around."

These thoughts would only be fleeting in Kathy's mind. Nonetheless they really upset her. She hated her mother for always being so negative, but worried that there might be an element of truth to what she said. But not tonight! She would not worry tonight. She loved Mike dearly, and tonight marked the end of their first year together.

By 5:30 Kathy had everything prepared and ready to be served. She quickly showered and put on the new dress she had gotten especially for tonight. At about 5:40 the phone rang. She hoped it wasn't Mike calling to say he'd be late; not tonight, please.

"Hello," she said anxiously.

"I'll bet he hasn't come home yet, has he?"

"No, mother," Kathy said, obviously annoyed.

"Did he at least call to say he'd be late?"

"Mother, I've got to go. Besides, I want to keep the line clear in case Mike needs to call. He'll be here, though."

At about 6:20, the phone rang again. This time Kathy was sure it was Mike. She was angry that he was calling to say he'd be late. She was also relieved that at least he was calling.

"Hello."

Unfortunately, it wasn't Mike afterall. Her secretary called to alert her that a judge changed her court time from 9:30 A.M. to 8:30 A.M. for tomorrow morning. She apologized for calling tonight as she realized how special it was, but knew Kathy would need this information as soon as possible.

Kathy was starting to worry. She glanced over at the table. The candle wax had dripped down on the tablecloth, and the wine was starting to lose its chill. Tears welled up in her eyes as she blew out the candles and put the wine back in the refrigerator. She thought about calling Mike at his office, but didn't want him to think she was checking up on him. She flipped through every magazine that was on their coffee table, filed her nails, and finished a bag of shelled peanuts.

"Oh, the hell with it," she thought. "Either something happened to him or else he forgot. Why did he have to forget?"

Within fifteen minutes, the table was cleared, the food was all wrapped and put away, and Kathy was in her pajamas and flannel robe. Now, she was prepared to wait.

At 9:30 she heard the key turn in the front door. The door opened and Mike walked into the den.

"Hi honey, what's for dinner?" Mike asked cheerfully.

Kathy ignored him. She tried to cover up her rage, but knew if she said anything she would be an open book.

"Kath, what's wrong?" Mike continued.

"Do you know what time it is?" she asked in a tone of voice that he could barely hear.

"Honey, what is the problem? Why are you giving me this cold treatment?"

"You really don't know, do you?" she asked almost as a challenge. "Where have you been? Do you have any idea what I've been doing since 8:30 this morning?"

"Kathy, I'm very tired. I don't know what the problem is. I don't know what I'm supposed to know and, to be honest, right now I really don't care. I'm hungry, I want to eat, and then I want to go to bed. I'm sorry, Kathy, but when you clam up on me and give me this silent treatment like your mother, I can't read your mind."

"How dare you compare me to my mother," she screamed back in rage. "My mother has nothing to do with this. Look on the mantle and see the card my mother remembered to send on a day that obviously means nothing to you."

Mike glanced at the mantle and was jarred when he realized the card meant he had forgotten their anniversary. "Kathy, I did forget. I am so sorry, honey. I've been so wrapped up in this

Slater account this week that it completely slipped my mind."

"Mike, why is it that everything comes before me?" she asked raising her voice.

"Come on, Kathy, don't make more out of this than it is. And lower your voice, the whole apartment complex will hear us."

"I don't give a damn about the apartment complex. Right now I give a damn about the fact that our marriage doesn't mean anything to you. Or maybe I should say that I don't mean anything to you."

"Kathy, listen," Mike pleaded.

"No, you listen," Kathy interrupted. "It's one thing that you forgot about today, but at least you could have called. Do you know what's been going through my mind since 6 o'clock tonight? I didn't know if you were in an accident or in bed with another woman. In fact, I still don't know for sure if you were with another woman. I purposely didn't call you at the office because I didn't want to seem like a nagging wife. But dammit Mike, not even a lousy call to say you were tied up!"

Mike was beginning to have a hard time staying calm. "You know, you think that just because you're the lawyer in the family and that your mother keeps reminding you that you're married to a salesman that I don't do anything important. Well let me tell you something, because I worked my tail off tonight I may end up closing an account that no one else has been able to touch. One way or another, you've got to rub it in that I don't have what it takes to be a doctor. You think doctors' wives complain if their husbands can't get to a phone?" By this point, Mike was out of breath from nearly screaming.

"I'm not married to a doctor, Mike. Besides that's not the point. You've got this stupid complex about being a salesman. Don't throw it up in my face. All right, so you didn't pass the medical entrance exams. Forget it already. I'm sick and tired of you bringing that up every time we fight about something. Regardless of whatever you were doing tonight, you could have broken away for five minutes to call me."

"So I didn't, so I forgot our anniversary, so I failed at that just like I failed the tests. Let's face it sweetie, you better decide if this is what you want, because you ain't going to get much more from me. Nothing I do is good enough for you and I'm getting sick of it. You treat me just like your mother has been stepping over your mealy mouthed father for the last umpteen years.

Well you may be like your mother, but I sure as hell am not
going to let you trample all over me."

"Stop it!" Kathy screamed.

"No, you stop it," Mike yelled in revenge. "When's the last time
you showed me the slightest bit of . . ."

Kathy didn't think she could take much more. Mike kept
pounding at her weak spot like a boxer hurling punches into his
opponent's wounds. Each time he mentioned her mother, she
felt her strength melting away. Her only defense was to fight
back using Mike's sensitivity about his test failures. She had
been so excited about giving him a beautiful dinner and evening.
She couldn't understand why they couldn't somehow work
things out.

AN ANALYSIS OF THE CASE STUDY

The superego is that part of the personality that inhibits the id from
driving the body into uncontrollable behavior. The superego's power
stems from one extremely potent emotion—anxiety. It is as though the
superego warns the ego that if it allows the id's emotions into awareness
or, even worse, gives up controls so that the id can act out its impulse,
then the superego will flood the ego with anxiety. If the id's powers do
get past the ego's controls, the superego delivers its punishment with
wrath and vengeance. The ego is consequently rendered inoperative. In
a very real sense then, the ego is trapped by a vicious cycle.

This cycle is illustrated by the situation with Kathy and Mike. Mike
was very late getting home and, moreover, didn't call to let Kathy know.
As a result, Kathy experienced many different feelings. She was worried
that he might have been involved in an accident, that he might be with
another woman, that he forgot their anniversary, and that whatever he
was involved in meant more to him than either she or their marriage
did.

Furthermore, as she worried about all of these possibilities, her
mother's voice echoed inside her head: "Mike isn't worth all the
aggravation," the voice said, and "Kathy, you have always regretted
when you haven't listened to me; don't throw your life away for this
boy." All of these worries and messages filled Kathy with a tremendous
amount of anxiety.

As Kathy waited for Mike to either come home or to call, she
convinced herself that Mike no longer loved her. She also repeated to

herself the messages from her mother that she was not capable of making her own decisions. Both of these messages were causing her ego to feel anxiety. In other words, instead of trying to get to the bottom of her emotions, she was allowing herself to be governed by them. As a result, she felt pain.

The id attempts to find a way of shutting off the pain through impulsive actions. Like the baby who screams to get food, Kathy screamed at Mike to relieve herself of the anxiety that she was experiencing. But it was not enough just to yell. Her id needed to provide Kathy with a means to protect herself against further hurt. To do this, Kathy's id used its forces to put Mike in pain so as to render him harmless. Kathy's id caused Mike to feel pain by flooding his ego with anxiety; in other words, she rendered his ego inoperative by taking away its ability to be in control. He was ashamed that he failed the medical school entrance exams. Her blow reached its target. His superego made his ego feel the pain of defeat. This anxiety rendered Mike's ego inoperative. It could not sustain itself against the barrage of punishment coming through Mike's superego as triggered by Kathy's id.

At this point, Mike's own id perceived that he was in pain. Since its job is to eliminate that pain and to protect Mike from further distress, Mike's id drove him to impulsively raise his voice and verbally attack Kathy. He knew exactly what to say so that her superego would flood her ego with anxiety. All he had to do was compare her to her mother.

This cycle continues to repeat itself over and over again. As long as the ego is rendered inoperative by the superego, it cannot function to bring about a reasonable settlement to the conflict. Each person becomes obsessed with hurting the other in order to make themselves feel better.

SUMMARY

Success in business largely depends on the leader's ability to get along with people. One of the reasons businesses fail is because of leaders who treat people more like objects than people—who not only have feelings, but who are capable of potent retaliation if those feelings are not understood and dealt with fairly.

This chapter has focused on the notion that a leader's power is heavily influenced by the natural forces of human temperament. The main objective of the body's biological and emotional operations is to maintain the level of internal balance that is vital to the continuance of life. Oftentimes, these personal needs take precedence over the objectives established by a business. During this conflict of interest, the business leader may resort to the use of the company's powers in order to impulsively relieve his or her own distress or to gratify self-directed pleasures.

The use of impulsive power violates the professional ethic. Preoccupied with internal tensions, the leader may fail to scrutinize words, actions, and deeds. Under the biological and emotional pressures of the id and superego, the leader may lose the capacities to arrive at rational decisions. The objectives of the business become secondary to the fulfillment of personal needs. Consequently, the leader might unknowingly place the future of the business in jeopardy.

Leadership becomes a type of paradox. A business must rely on leadership to meet its objectives. Yet leaders, as human beings, are subject to the homeostatic programming of their human temperament. The solution to this paradox requires that leaders maintain a conscious vigilance over their own internal programming to prevent it from interfering with the needs of the company. This vigilance involves:

1. Getting the ego operational before the tensions build to a level where they have enough strike force to render it inoperative.
2. Building the technical and adaptive capacities of the ego so that it can calm the anxieties of the superego and rechannel the urges from the id into ideas and thoughts that can be satisfied with reason and understanding.

The process of using judicious power in leadership depends on the development of the capacity to reason during periods of intense frustration and tension. Effective leaders are people who understand vulnerabilities as areas that are rooted within the id and superego. These systems can be sometimes very easily triggered within the people with whom leaders work. If leadership is based on domination and intimidation, leaders will at some point have to reckon with the ids and superegos of the people they dominate and intimidate. On the other hand, if leaders can shore up their own egos by learning to minimize the damaging effects from id and superego, they will be in a position to base their leadership on sound judgment rather than on reactive and aggressive emotions. Furthermore, if they can learn how to soothe the id and superego of subordinates, they will be in a position to help them function within their own ego.

The Relationship Life Cycle can provide a model to help a leader understand how the members of a work team can use conflict to strengthen commitment to one another as well as to the organization itself. Once leaders recognize the presence of conflict, they can redirect energies from defensive and self-serving behaviors into discussion that can help to reclarify roles and redefine expectations.

Effective and productive leadership stems from a well-developed and strongly reinforced ego—an ego that can actively cope with the powers of the id and superego, that can withstand the tensions and pressures barraging it from the id and superego, and that can facilitate the effective operation of the ego within the members of a work team.

TOPICS FOR DISCUSSION

1. Discuss how the Relationship Life Cycle could be applied to account for difficulties that leaders might experience with and among their followers.
2. Using the Relationship Life Cycle as a model, what measures could a leader take to resolve conflicts on the work team?
3. Discuss the ways in which a leader's powers are largely dependent upon human nature.
4. Defend the concept that human behavior follows logical principles.
5. Define homeostasis and describe its relationship to human temperament.
6. What have the concepts of the Relationship Life Cycle and the behavior operating system taught you about people?

RECOMMENDED READINGS

HALL, C. (1954). *A primer of freudian psychology*. New York: Mentor.

HARRIS, T. (1967). *I'm okay-You're okay*. New York: Avon.

HUNTER, E. (1956). *Brainwashing: The story of men who defied it*. New York: Farrar, Straus and Cudany.

MACLEAN, P. (1958). The limbic system with respect to self-preservation and the preservation of the species. *Journal of Nervous and Mental Disease, 127* (1), 1–11.

NEWSWEEK (1983, February 7). The mysteries of the brain. pp. 40–49.

PAPEZ, J. W. (1937, October). A proposed mechanism of emotion. *Archives of Neurology and Psychiatry, 38*, 725–743.

RESTAK, R. (1984). *The Brain*. New York: Bantam.

SCHEFLIN, A., & OPTON, E. (1978). *The mind manipulators*. New York: Paddington Press.

SMITH, L. (1976). *Improving your child's brain chemistry*. New York: Pocket Books.

CHAPTER THREE
EMOTIONAL STABILITY IN LEADERSHIP

OUTLINE

MAJOR CONCEPTS
INTRODUCTION

The Case of Dr. Kramer
Analysis of the Case Study
The Identification and Management of Superego Triggers
Time Management
Physical Activity
Relaxation

SUMMARY
TOPICS FOR DISCUSSION
RECOMMENDED READINGS

MAJOR CONCEPTS

1. Leaders must be able to integrate the natural forces of their own emotional demands with the ability to remain clear headed under the pressure and strain of organizational responsibility.

2. One of the most reliable indexes of emotional maturity is how a person copes with pressure. People who are emotionally stable cope with pressure by thinking through the options rather than impulsively defending their own self-directed interests.

3. A *superego trigger* is any event that causes a person to feel anxious, vulnerable, threatened, or helpless.

4. The greater degree of emotional stability that we have, the more likely we will be to disperse superego anxiety into channels for clear thinking.

5. Superego triggers can flood the ego with anxiety when a person is physically stressed such as from fatigue, illness, hunger, and so forth. They can also flood the ego with anxiety through comments or gestures that an individual perceives as a personal attack.

6. Superego triggers have the effect of making you feel caught off guard and left out of control. They provoke you into feeling like you must defend yourself.

7. The process of becoming aware of this feeling is actually a first step toward making a transition from your superego into your ego rather than shutting down the ego and moving into your id.

8. Accessing and maintaining the functions of the ego depend specifically on the process of organized thinking.

9. *Discretionary time* is the time that you can plan. It is similar to budgeting your money.

10. *Response time* is that period during which you must respond to events spontaneously and without adequate preparation.

11. Exercise that increases the muscle's ability to intake and use oxygen is called *aerobic exercise*. Its purpose is to develop a muscular system that can efficiently take in oxygen and can eliminate the toxic byproducts of bodily activities.

12. The process of deep relaxation involves tensing a muscle nearly to an extreme (though not to the point of pain), holding the tension, and then abruptly releasing the tension.

13. One of the most effective methods for releasing tension is called *internal free association*.

INTRODUCTION

Chapter 2 presented a framework for understanding how human temperament can affect productivity in working relationships. To enhance the capacity to apply that knowledge, leaders must be able to integrate the natural forces of their own emotional demands with the ability to remain clear headed under the pressure and strain of organizational responsibility. This skill, so uniquely important to effective leadership, links directly with emotional maturity. In this chapter, we will be considering procedures that you can learn in order to access and maintain control over your ego. Recall from Chapter 2 that the ego is that part of the personality that enables you to solve problems through the process of reasoning and judgment rather than impulsive and aggressive actions. The procedures that we will be considering are time management, physical activity, and relaxation. The objective of each set of procedures is to help you desensitize anxieties that could otherwise interfere with your ability to think, reason, and make sound decisions.

In his book *Secrets of a Corporate Headhunter*, John Wareham (1980) wrote that it is very risky to assume a person is emotionally mature. Many immature people, Wareham claimed, can seduce you into an adultlike relationship through childlike charm and their lifelong ability to distract your attention away from their shortcomings. This type of person is concerned with only his immediate gratification and

> . . . tends to see his employer as a sort of Santa Claus: what he wants is to have someone to look after him just like his mommy and daddy did.*

The clues that Wareham (1980) suggests indicate emotional maturity are:

1. The extent of genuine concern for the welfare of other people in terms of his willingness to put his own needs aside for the welfare of the work team.
2. The stability of his previous business conduct as it reflects his judgment, his impulses, his consideration for the present and the future.
3. The soundness of his financial judgments in terms of how they reflect adult-level thinking in a cool, level-headed way.

*John Wareham, excerpted from *Secrets of a Corporate Headhunter*. Copyright © 1980 The Wareham Family Trust. Reprinted with permission of Athenuem Publishers, Inc.

4. The manner in which he relates to the members of his family as he is directly observed in social situations as well as the way in which he discusses them during working hours.
5. The avenues through which he channels his anger; stories about how other people were to blame, were unreasonable, or stood in his way of success can suggest that his own hostilities are all too frequently displaced on others.

One of the most reliable indexes of emotional maturity is how a person copes with pressure. People who are emotionally stable cope with pressure by thinking through the options rather than impulsively defending their own self-directed interests.

The case study that follows involves a physician who is challenged to support his opinion to a patient after that patient consulted another doctor for a second opinion. Decide for yourself whether or not this physician can be considered an emotionally stable person. Here is a clue:

> John Ruskin once said that pride is at the bottom of all great mistakes. (Weber, 1980)

The Case of Dr. Kramer

It was unmistakable. She told herself it was nothing; probably just something that would go away in a day or two. But it still haunted her. Tina Hopkins found a hard, roundish lump in her right breast. She stood in front of the mirror night after night tracing it's shape with her index finger, trying to pretend it wasn't there. But it was. Tina was thirty-two. After getting divorced six months ago, she decided to return to graduate school to finish a master's degree in architecture. Lately, she had been almost totally unable to concentrate on her studies. She told Dr. Kramer, a surgeon who had come highly recommended, that she had never had a breast lump before. "My best friend lost her mother to cancer. It started from this kind of thing," Tina said, "and I can't help but feel that I'm living with some sort of time bomb that sooner or later is going to explode."

Dr. Kramer took meticulous notes as Tina answered his questions about her medical history. He listened with a great deal of warmth and compassion. His manner during the physical examination exuded a strength, a certainty that only years of experience could have cultivated. He carefully explored the lump from every angle. Then he explained that he was going to stick a needle in it to see if any fluid could be drained out. As he finished, he gently patted her on the shoulder and said they could talk in his office in the next few minutes. Tina quivered while she dressed herself trying to control her anxiety over what Dr. Kramer was about to tell her. She dreaded his confirmation that she would have to be admitted to the hospital for surgery.

His office was just next door. She knocked softly. He told her to come in and sit down. Just then his phone rang and he took the call. She watched him as he flipped through another patient's chart. Apparently, he was speaking to another doctor.

"Yes, John, the laporoscopy reveals chronic endometriosis. Your suspicions were right on the money. Yes, I've told her and she has already agreed to surgery. Well, if she wants to have kids, it's the only chance she's got. She wasn't crazy about the idea of major surgery, but when I told her she'd still be able to wear a bikini, she came around. Sure, I . . ."

Amidst her anxiety, Tina liked Dr. Kramer. She felt protected by him. She listened to him as he discussed the other patient on the phone. His voice was deep, gentle, soothing. He fit well in his office of rich walnut panels, a huge oak desk, and certificates up and down two of the walls. She was beginning to feel much better about hearing whatever he was about to tell her.

"Thanks for the referral, John. Sure, let's get together for lunch next week. Fine, bye now." He put the phone down, closed the other patient's file, and began reviewing Tina's.

As he pondered the notes, he began explaining, "The lump appears to be the size of a small peanut. I extracted a little fluid from it, which is a good sign. I really don't think it's anything to worry about."

At that point, he made a few more notes, closed the file, and then put it in his "out" basket. "On your way out, Tina, tell the receptionist to schedule a return visit in two months."

Tina reached for her purse, got up from the chair, and started to walk toward the door. She hesitated for a moment and then asked, "Isn't two months kind of long to wait, shouldn't I be coming back sooner than that?"

He walked around from behind his desk, reached around and put his arm around her shoulder. "Now Tina, I don't want you to worry. That's the worst thing you can do. Now go on about your little life and just forget that it's there. Come back again in two months and we'll take another look, okay?"

It was really more of an order than a question, she thought. She was amazed at how many different feelings she experienced toward this man in the course of her appointment with him. "Who does he think he is," she screamed in silence to herself, "telling me to forget that it's there. How can any woman be expected to forget that there is a lump in her breast? Get on with my little life, he tells me. He's made me so mad that at least I've forgotten how scared I was."

The next examination was over almost before it started. Dr. Kramer reviewed his notes and then traced the outline of the lump.

"It hasn't changed at all," he explained to Tina. "I want to see you again after your next period. Looks like about three weeks from now. Hang in there."

As he got up to leave, Tina heard herself blurting out, "Wait, Dr. Kramer, I don't mean to be rude, but I don't feel like you've told me anything. I can't just be expected to wait day after day while this thing is growing inside of me. I'm not sleeping or eating, I can't concentrate on my studies. Isn't there anything you can do, now?"

His warmth seemed to return almost immediately. "Sure," he said. He sat back down and wrote out a prescription. "I want you to take one of these every four hours and make sure you take one before bedtime." Tina gratefully took the prescription and asked, "Will they dissolve the lump?"

He looked puzzled. "Dissolve the lump?" he asked. "No, of course not," he replied impatiently. "They're tranquilizers to calm you down and help you sleep."

She felt her heart race as she tried to fold the paper and put it in her purse. Two months she had waited for this appointment. Now, she wouldn't know any more until after her next period. Irregular as she had been since the divorce, that might not be for another six weeks. She refused to wait around helplessly. She decided to see her gynecologist for his opinion. Fortunately, a patient canceled an appointment and her gynecologist, Dr. Mills, was able to see Tina within about 45 minutes. She carefully explained what had happened during the last two appointments with Dr. Kramer. Dr. Mills spoke highly of him.

"He's a fine surgeon. Did you know he's on the board of several hospitals in town and he's running for president of our state medical society."

Dr. Mills was about to continue when Tina interrupted. "But what do you think?" she insisted.

He didn't answer right away. He reexamined the area for a third time and then replied. "Tina, I don't feel anything about the lump that would make me suspicious. But then, I could be wrong. A doctor never knows for certain just on the basis of the physical examination."

"Well, isn't there anything else that can be done to find out for sure?" she asked. "Shouldn't I have exploratory surgery; can't they biopsy it?"

"If you were at high risk, yes, but since neither your medical history, your family background, nor your physical findings gives indications of cancerous conditions, surgery is not the next step," Dr. Mills explained. He went on. "What I would like you to consider is a mammogram."

"A what?" Tina asked.

"A mammogram," he repeated. "It's a special kind of x-ray of the breast. In fact, it's probably a good idea to have both breasts done to give us a basis of comparison for now and for the future. The results would give us a pretty clear indication as to whether or not a malignancy is present. Now remember," he reiterated, "I do not believe there is. Some patients think that just because we order a test that we believe there may be cancer. Most definitely, Tina, that is not the case. But since I can't be absolutely sure, a mammogram can give us much more information. If the radiologist's interpretation is negative, you'll sleep a lot easier. If by some chance it is positive, at least we'll know now instead of waiting another three to six weeks for your next surgical visit."

Tina felt immediate relief. At least she could do something right away to get to the facts.

Dr. Mills asked if she would like him to notify Dr. Kramer that a mammogram was being ordered through a local radiology lab.

"No," she told him. She would tell Dr. Kramer herself. She reached Dr. Kramer's office only to be put on hold for what seemed like ten to twelve minutes. Finally, Dr. Kramer picked up the phone.

"This is Dr. Kramer . . ."

Tina hesitated and then told him of her visit to Dr. Mills and about her decision to have the mammogram.

He replied instantly. "A mammogram! You are not a candidate for a mammogram."

Tina quickly felt herself becoming intimidated. She tried to explain what Dr. Mills had told her, but the words just wouldn't come out. Dr. Kramer cut off the attempt.

"Obviously, Dr. Mills is unfamiliar with the latest research. The radiological journals have made it clear that mammograms should not be used on women under 40. The risk from the radiation doesn't warrant the benefit."

The line went silent for a few seconds. Tina wanted to convince him that a mammogram was the right thing to do, but now he had confused her. Her confidence in Dr. Mills began to buckle under the force of Dr. Kramer's recital. "But at least I'd know one way or the other," she pleaded. "I'd know something. At least I could do something."

Dr. Kramer's voice then took on the tones of a prosecutor cross-examining a defendant. "Are you the doctor or am I? If I thought a mammogram had been indicated, I would have ordered it. The lump in your breast gives no palpable signs of being malignant. You are overreacting to it which is why I told you to take those tranquilizers. Now when is your next appointment?"

Tina had all she could do to get any voice to come out of her mouth, let alone to collect her thoughts. "You told me to call your office and set up an appointment after my next period," she replied.

"Well, see that you do just that," he admonished. "And in the meantime," he continued, "make up your mind who your doctor is. If it's Dr. Mills, so be it. Get the mammogram. But if you want me to treat you, stop this senseless worrying, forget the mammogram, and stop running all over town to different doctors. Now call me after your next period and I'll take another look at it for you."

When she finally let go of the receiver, she realized how much her hand hurt from clenching the phone so tight. She immediately took out the bottle of tranquilizers from her purse and gulped two down with a glass of water. Aside from everything he had told her, Dr. Kramer essentially wanted her to believe that Dr. Mills didn't know what he was talking about, that the mammogram could actually cause cancer even if the breast lump was benign. She was totally confused by the contradictions between the two physicians and felt badly humiliated by Dr. Kramer. She even felt guilty and worried that she had made a fool of Dr. Mills to this "fine surgeon" that the whole medical community had been raving about.

She decided to call Dr. Mills to tell him what had happened. He let her talk for a long while, interrupting only with gentle reassurances for her to continue.

When she finished, he replied, "You know, I can understand Dr. Kramer's concern. The research in the radiological journals states very clearly that women under the age of 40 should not be given mammograms for the purpose of routine screening. At one point, we hoped mammograms could be as much a part of a gynecological checkup as taking blood pressure is. You see, many women don't check themselves for breast lumps. So we all hoped that the mammogram, like the pap smear, would be an almost failsafe mechanism for detection. Unfortunately, because of the fact that any x-ray carries a certain amount of cancer-inducing risk due to radiation exposure, the routine use of mammograms for screening purposes was abandoned. You, on the other hand, have already performed the screening portion of the exam by finding the lump yourself. Your case at this point is clearly beyond the screening stage. The mammogram can give us a pretty good indication as to whether or not that lump is cancerous. Now, what about the risk? You have every right to know about it. Out of every million women who at the time of the mammogram did not have breast cancer, one of those women will develop breast cancer from exposure to the radiation in the mammogram. Under the circumstances, I would advise you to have the procedure done."

Tina thought over what he had just explained to her. She appreciated the detail and the respect he had shown her. There was no doubt in her mind that he knew what he was talking about. One question remained for her to ask. Perhaps it was unfair, but considering the risk, she needed to know how he would answer. "Given the same set of physical findings, Dr. Mills . . . what would you tell your wife?"

Without hesitation he said, "I would tell her to have the mammogram."

Tina thanked him and hung up the phone. The tranquilizers were making her drowsy. Nonetheless, her mind was clear enough to appreciate the details that Dr. Mills had just given her. The fact that he took the time to give her such an extensive explanation went a long way toward easing her anxieties. Not only did he give her a good deal of information, but he did so with personal warmth as well as with respect for his colleague; even after he learned that such respect was not given him.

Tina decided to have the mammogram. The results were negative. The breast lump, by all indications, was not cancerous. Dr. Kramer's experience as a surgeon had been confirmed after all.

ANALYSIS OF THE CASE STUDY

Was Dr. Kramer an emotionally stable person? The answer is a qualified "maybe." Certainly, we would imagine that for anyone to succeed in becoming a surgeon, a high degree of emotional maturity is an absolute necessity. However, given a particular set of circumstances, the ability to keep in control of one's emotions could collapse. In Dr. Kramer's case, we can say that the way that Tina talked to him appeared to threaten his emotional stability. Compared to the warmth and reassurance that he showed toward Tina initially, he later scolded and intimidated her. Was he perhaps using good medical judgment as yet another way for treating her condition? That possibility is somewhat remote. He appeared to be genuinely threatened by her decision to question his judgment. It was at that point that he became threatened. In other words, his pride influenced his behavior.

The problem that Dr. Kramer experienced is common to all of us at one time or another. When Tina raised questions about his method of treating her, Dr. Kramer became anxious. To return to the terminology from Chapter 2, his superego flooded his ego with anxiety. His ego could not disperse the anxiety into channels for clear thinking. Instead, it shut down. Subsequently, the id perceived that emotional pain was present in the mental framework and interpreted it as a threat to homeostasis. Since its job is to remove such threats, it responded by steering available energies into impulsive outlets.

THE IDENTIFICATION AND MANAGEMENT OF SUPEREGO TRIGGERS

A *superego trigger* is any event that causes a person to feel anxious, vulnerable, threatened, or helpless. The way that we respond to superego triggers is related to just how emotionally stable we are. The greater the amount of emotional stability that we have, the more likely we will be to disperse superego anxiety into channels for clear thinking. In other words, we will be able to access our ego to manage the problem. The smaller the amount of emotional stability that we have, the less likely we will be to access our ego. Instead, our ego will not be able to manage the anxiety. Our id will perceive that our homeostasis is threatened, and it will subsequently steer our energies into impulsive and aggressive behaviors.

Superego triggers have the effect of making you feel caught off-guard and left out of control. They provoke you into feeling like you must defend yourself. The process of becoming aware of this feeling is actually a first step toward making a transition from your superego into your ego rather than shutting down the ego and moving into your id. When you find that you are feeling irritable, tired, tense, frustrated, impatient, rushed, aggravated, threatened, insecure, anxious, over-whelmed, envious, or experiencing any related feelings, let the awareness of these feelings sink in. This awareness is your first insight that your ego is beginning to shut down. Do something about it before you become impulsive. Put the feeling into words and say them to yourself. This process helps to restore the operations of your ego so that you can take some rational measures to prevent impulsive actions that you might well regret later.

There are steps you can take to reduce your vulnerability to the superego trigger. Each step involves reducing your sensitivity to stress and pressure. They are time management, physical activity, and relaxation training.

Time Management

Accessing and maintaining the functions of the ego depend specifically on the process of organized thinking. One major way to organize your thinking and maintain it that way is to consistently practice two simple concepts of time management: (1) discretionary time and (2) response time (Weber, 1980).

Discretionary time. *Discretionary time* is the time that you can plan, and it is similar to budgeting your money. Your activities are divided into categories in terms of priority; the categories are then scheduled into time slots that are earmarked for each category.

You will need a few simple tools to use discretionary time management:

1. A job-list binder
2. A day-scheduling binder
3. A five-year calendar
4. Two yearly storage binders

The purpose of the *job-list binder* is to enable you to write down, in a manner that is highly organized and consistent, the "jobs" that you must either get done yourself or delegate. The heart of the system is a carbonless set of two 8½ by 11 sheets of paper. You can buy these sets in bulk through any paper distribution house. Have them collated and three-hole punched and then printed according to the format described below. Then simply insert them into any standard three-ring binder and label it "Job-List Binder (current)."

Within each set, the top sheet is the original (usually white) and the bottom sheet is the copy (usually pink or yellow). Each sheet is divided into four sections. On the original sheet of each set, the sections are separated by a perforated line and on the copy sheet the sections are separated by a dashed line.

Each section is called a "job-listing." At the top of the job listing are lines for entering the job number and the job title. The job number is a number that combines the day's date with the number of the job that is being listed for that particular day. For example, the number of the second job entered in the job-list binder on August 2, 1984, would be 080284-2. The job title identifies the job by a one- to three-word description.

Immediately below the top line is space for specifying the steps that must be taken to accomplish the job. At the bottom of the section is a line that calls for identifying the person who is to accomplish the job, the absolute deadline, and a review date.

After recording all of this information, you would then tear off the completed section at the perforation on the original sheet within the two-part set. At that point, you would give the "job ticket" to whomever you have assigned to complete that particular job (see Appendix A).

The job-list binder has all of the advantages of an ordinary "to-do" list. With the job-list binder, however, you have additional advantages. First, the job-list binder is organized. By keeping the binder with you during travel and appointments, you can enter job assignments the moment you think of them. You don't have to rely on your memory later on to retrieve any details that you had previously worked out mentally. The entries are recorded in the order you think of them, and they contain all the most pertinent information you will later need to see that the job is completed. Second, unlike a "to-do" list that may be made on a scrap of paper, the job-list binder contains important documents and, therefore, would not be easily misplaced. Third, the entries help you monitor the progress of the job. By periodically reviewing pages from previous days' entries, you will have detailed reminders of which jobs you have instigated as well as those jobs that you have conveniently "forgotten about." Finally, the job-list binder provides you with records of just what jobs you have planned, abandoned, and accomplished over any given period of time (see yearly storage binders). Reviewing these records could easily document both the quantity and the quality of your work, thus serving as data to justify your worth to the company.

Just as the job-list binder can be compared to the "to-do" list, the *day-scheduling binder* can be compared to an appointment book. The main purpose of the day-scheduling binder is to enable you to schedule your time. The schedule revolves around your actual workday; however, you plan your schedule both on a short-term and a long-term basis.

The day-scheduling binder is composed of four sections. Each represents one quarter of the calendar year. The pages within each of the four sections are color coded so that each quarter is represented by a different color. Each page is identified by the day, month, and year. In every other way, the pages within each of the sections are identical.

The top half of the page looks like the pages in many conventional appointment books. There are two columns with half-hour time slots that run consecutively from 7:00 A.M. to 9:00 P.M. The bottom half of the page is blank. Within this space is where you will determine which jobs you will need to accomplish on this particular day and how much time each will require. By referring back to your job-list binder, you will know what jobs are waiting to be scheduled and how many of them you can fit in for that particular day. As you schedule appointments during the upcoming days and weeks in the quarter, you can arrange them with the knowledge that you have been and will continue to be aware of the assignments from the job-list binder that you are monitoring. By coordinating the day-scheduling binder with the job-list binder, you establish and remain in control of the planning, expenditure, and recording of your discretionary time.

Earlier, we mentioned that the tools for managing discretionary time also included a five-year calendar and two yearly storage binders. We'll now look at both of these additional tools.

The purpose of the *five-year calendar* is simply as a reference in scheduling your work assignments. Any single sheet that lists the months by year over a five-year period will work quite well. You can simply insert it into your day-scheduling binder so that you can have immediate access to it for quick reference.

The *two yearly storage binders* are for maintaining a permanent record of your inactive job-list records and your day-scheduling records, respectively. At the end of each quarter, insert the records into their appropriate yearly storage binders. Then at the end of each year, shelve the records for that year making sure that you have appropriately titled and dated each of the binders. You can then begin storage binders for the upcoming year.

Response Time

Response time is that time over which you have far less control compared to discretionary time. The name "response time" itself implies that you will be "responding" to situations rather than planning them. In discretionary time, you have much more ability to establish and remain in control of situations. You make decisions that will structure the events. You decide, in advance, whom you will see, how much time you will spend, and just what objectives you intend to accomplish. For the most part, you can plan just about how everything will occur. Response time is much different.

Usually, response time occurs in the form of interruptions and/or unplanned interactions. The interruptions may be unexpected phone calls, "urgent messages," or an office visitor needing your immediate attention. The unplanned interaction might be someone needing to talk to you outside of your office—perhaps in the elevator, on a break, in the parking garage, or possibly even in some sort of social setting. Such interruptions and unplanned interactions involve discussion of a business matter and may culminate in making an important decision.

Response time carries with it significant risks. First of all, since the interaction that occurs during response time was not expected, you are not prepared for it. Your mind has been on other matters. Consequently, you must tune out the matter to which you had been attending and tune in to the matter at hand. As such, you will not likely be as alert to all the significant issues regarding the new matter as you would have been had you had time to prepare for it. In addition, interruptions tend to be somewhat intrusive. Although you may not overtly show it, you will likely feel at least mildly annoyed. In other words, the interruption will probably trigger your superego, which in turn will fire up your id.

Before we look at ways to cope with the problems of response time, we must consider one more of its serious complications. Under the most ideal circumstances, two people are seldom consistent in the ways they perceive and remember the details and events of a situation. All too often person A says, "But you said you would do _____ ," while person B says, "I'm sorry, you're mistaken, I never said any such thing, it was just the opposite."

For a variety of reasons, situations are often resolved by people who think they are in agreement. When the time comes for the decisions to be implemented, however, the parties involved sometimes discover that there has been a misunderstanding. The resultant feelings range from disappointment to deep anger and resentment.

These forms of misunderstanding nearly always stem from interactions that occur as a part of response time. Because one or both of the parties have been involved in the processing of some other matter, they usually do not attend to response time matters with the detail needed to avert a later complication.

One way to cope with response time is to plan for it as much as possible. Instead of allowing yourself to be caught offguard, anticipate the unexpected, jot it down in your job-list binder, and then schedule it out through your daily-scheduling binder. Many people even build in a certain amount of "crisis time" into their daily schedule. In that way, when you are barraged with a number of unexpected phone calls that you cannot turn away, you can take the time to attend to them; you have budgeted extra time later on when you can return to the original matter you had been working on before the interruptions occurred.

The second strategy to cope with response time is the most crucial. Judicious and consistent use of the method to be presented below will significantly minimize the risk of short circuits to your ego for weeks, months, and even years beyond the time you actually put it into operation. The method itself is very simple. It merely requires that you make notes of each situation in which you have a business interaction.

The notes are entered in the *response time binder*. Similar to the job-list binder, in the response time binder are sets of carbonless paper. Each set is composed of an original (white) and a copy (yellow or pink) 8½ by 11 sheet. On each sheet are four sections. The sections on the original sheet are separated by perforated lines and the sections on the copy sheet are separated by dotted lines. There are a sufficient number of sets in each binder to meet the needs of entries for each calendar quarter.

Each of the four sections on the page is designed to enable you to enter your notes from a response time interaction. The top line contains space for noting the date, the time at which the interaction began, the name of the person with whom you had the interaction, and the file to which the interaction relates. For example, you might enter 08-23-83, 8:45 A.M., R. Hennesey, Roosner Project. Below the top line is a space of two inches within which you can enter your notes of the interaction. The time to enter the notes is *immediately* after the interaction has been completed or as soon thereafter as possible. Within the space write down the following information:

1. Who initiated the interaction?
2. In what setting did the interaction occur (phone, your office, other's office, baseball stadium, etc.)?
3. Why was the interaction initiated? *Be specific.*
    a. What does the other person want?
    b. What do you want?
4. What action was taken or will be taken?—*Be specific.*
    a. Who agreed to do what?
    b. By when?

For example:

> R. Hennesey called me to find out if he could be excused from the Roosner board meeting. I asked what the reason was for his intended absence. He informed me that the section auditor needed to consult with him during the time when the Roosner board meeting would be in session. I told him that he could be excused if he sent me a report one week prior to the meeting that summarized his division's activities so that I could present it to the Roosner board on his behalf. He agreed.

In the bottom right corner of each section is a space that calls for an entry of the time at which the interaction ended. Once you have completed your notations, simply tear off the record at the perforation. File the record of the original in the file that you identified on the form. In the case of the above example, the record would be filed in the Roosner file. You could also make a photocopy of the original and place it in the file you might keep for the person with whom you had the interaction, if as in this case the person and the project are different. The copy (the second sheet in the set) remains in the response time binder, to provide you with a chronological record of the interactions during that particular period.

For the small price of a few minutes of your time, you are protecting yourself against details you might otherwise forget. The response time binder will give you immediate access to your on-the-spot recollection of the events that transpired during what might have been a frenzied time. Although your intent is not necessarily to prove yourself right and the other person wrong, it is difficult for another person to argue with a written record, especially a record that is substantiated with an abundance of specific details.

In addition to providing you with documentation of the nature and results of interactions, the response time binder offers you a record of interactions for individual people, for any number of people for specific projects, and for all the interactions in which you were involved during any given period of time. Your ability to retrieve information will be immediate, and the accuracy of the information will be firm and substantial.

Finally, and perhaps most important, because you will have access to your response time records, you will be in a position of simply reporting the events that occurred. Even if the actual interaction took place months or even years ago, your report will contain details that vividly reconstruct its events. You will be in control of the situation. By having used the functions of your ego (recording the events that occurred as a part of the interaction immediately after they happened), you will be able to document, substantiate, and justify any actions that you had taken or may yet have to implement regarding the situation. Above all, your actions will be completely governed by the operations of your ego.

Physical Activity

Research has linked exercise with improvements in a variety of medical conditions; it also helps in weight control, reduces pain from common forms of headache, reduces nervous tension, and contributes to a general sense of well-being. The conclusions from one study indicated that a 15-minute walk can provide more relaxation than a tranquilizer (Mirkin & Hoffman, 1978).

Science has not yet firmly established why exercise improves mood, although several theories are under investigation. One is related to a hormone known as norepinephrine. This hormone is one of the brain's neurochemical transmitters that carry electrical impulses throughout the circuits of the nervous system. The presumption is that exercise increases the levels of norepinephrine, which in effect supports the operations of the ego. Other theories contend that exercise improves mood by increasing the oxygen supplies to the brain, by reducing salt levels thereby increasing perspiration to rid the body of toxins, and by promoting deep levels of sleep (Mirkin & Hoffman, 1978).

The term *aerobic* refers to the way in which a muscle consumes oxygen during the process of burning fuel for muscular contraction. This fuel is composed of glycogen (sugar) and fat. To be converted to energy this fuel must be burned, a process that requires oxygen. The oxygen is delivered to the muscles through red blood cells within the general circulation of blood throughout the body. If sufficient levels of oxygen are available to the muscle, the byproducts of wastes resulting from contraction are eliminated from the body through carbon dioxide during exhalation. However, muscles with insufficient amounts of oxygen cannot rid themselves of toxic byproducts. Subsequently, these toxins accumulate in the muscles and eventually spill over into the bloodstream. The result is bodily fatigue. Exercise that increases the muscle's ability to intake and use oxygen is called *aerobic exercise*. Its purpose is to develop a muscular system that can efficiently intake oxygen and can eliminate the toxic byproducts of bodily activities (Mirkin & Hoffman, 1978).

The main objective of aerobic conditioning is to increase the maximum volume of oxygen that the body can intake and use at any given time. The central focus of this conditioning is the heart and lungs. Dr. Kenneth H. Cooper (1977, 1972), Director of the Institute for Aerobic Research, has reported on the numerous anatomic and biochemical benefits that occur as a result of aerobic conditioning. These effects include:

1. Strengthening the respiratory muscles and reducing the resistance to airflow so as to increase the flow of air in and out of the lungs.
2. Increasing the pumping capacity of the heart to deliver more oxygen to organs and tissues throughout the body.
3. Developing greater muscle tone that contributes to improved general circulation and to lowering blood pressure.
4. Increasing overall blood circulation as well as the number of red blood cells so that the blood can more effectively deliver oxygen throughout the body.

Aerobic exercise can be any form of physical activity that accomplishes this objective. By nature, aerobic exercise will be vigorous, sustained, and repetitive—such as running, swimming, and cycling. Dr. Cooper's research indicates that the majority of people who condition themselves aerobically can reach at least minimum levels of fitness for their particular age categories.

For many people, the most difficult part of exercising is overcoming the resistance to start and stick with an exercise program. From the perspective of human temperament, this resistance can be viewed as the id's attempt to eliminate potential discomfort. Once this resistance is overcome and a person exercises vigorously and regularly, the results are almost universally rewarding. The very practical objective is to "feel good" as a result of the exercise program. Your elevated mood will be a reflection of the increased operational capacities of your cortex. You will have more energy available for rational thinking, and there will be less need for impulsive reactions.

It is beyond the scope of this book to include or endorse specific exercise programs. Regardless of the specific program, most reputable authors urge the participant to precede participation with a thorough physical examination and to begin the program only after obtaining the consent of a physician. The sooner you begin and the more regularly you exercise, the greater capacities you will develop for self-control.

Relaxation

In comparing the body to a machine, it is easy to see that maximum performance depends upon adequate maintenance. As an instrument of nature, the body is composed of systems all of which are interconnected and function according to a precisely tuned mechanism of checks and balances. Substitute table sugar for carbohydrates and energy may be rapid, but short-lived. Disregard exercise in favor of sedentary pleasure and the following day of work could be ruled by fatigue and loss of temper.

The prospective and even the experienced leader cannot overlearn the importance of maintaining the body's system of homeostasis. Left to the automatic functions of the hypothalamus, the body's internal balance will inevitably be maintained through the forces of the id and the superego. By carefully attending to the ongoing demands of homeostasis, the ego can maintain conscious control of the forces required for the judicious management of power in leadership. In addition to monitoring the body's physical needs through exercise and controlled nutrition, the ego can also provide for the systematic release of bodily tensions through periodic repetitions of progressive relaxation.

The process of deep relaxation involves tensing a muscle nearly to an extreme—though not to the point of pain—holding the tension, and then abruptly releasing the tension. At the moment the tension is released, you can appreciate a very comforting feeling of relaxation at the muscle site.

Try this process now. Clench your right fist as hard as you can . . . harder . . . harder . . . hold the tension . . . hold it . . . now, let go. Feel the tremendous difference. Your right hand feels a great relief, and the relaxation lingers within its muscles as you enjoy the contrast between the tension and the relief from this tension.

The method of muscle tensing and relaxing was developed by a psychologist many years ago (Jacobson, 1962). He reasoned that the body could not experience states of tension and relaxation at the same time. In other words, a patient could be relieved of tension if taught how to relax. The method became known as "progressive relaxation." Used by a psychologist as a form of psychotherapy, the patient was instructed to alternately tense a muscle followed by instructions to relax the muscle. Usually the procedure follows a sequence that begins with the muscles in the lower extremities and moves upward along the body until the patient has relaxed most of the major muscles in the feet, legs, abdomen and buttocks, chest and back, shoulders and arms, neck, and the face. The term *progressive* relates to how the relaxation literally progresses throughout the entire body from toes to head.

As a method for harmlessly discharging tension from the id, progressive relaxation works extremely well. By the time you have completed a 20-minute progressive relaxation session, your body will be totally relaxed. Tensions that had been stored in muscles throughout your body that might have otherwise triggered impulsive reactions from the id or that might have been locked within the muscles by the superego will be comfortably removed. You will experience a feeling of warmth and calm very similar to what you feel just after a deep and prolonged yawn.

A second use for progressive relaxation is to relieve specific instances of tension and anxiety. For example, if you are anxious about confronting a co-worker regarding a conflict that has been brewing between the two of you for some time, an abbreviated session of progressive relaxation would help you harmlessly discharge tension from your id and enable you to access your ego.

Deep relaxation is effective because it enables the id to do its job (discharge tension) in a manner that doesn't trigger the superego. In that way, the ego has sufficient stores of energy available for its own operation, namely to solve problems on the basis of reason.

Many people use a form of progressive relaxation as a means to fall asleep. In combination with progressive relaxation, one of the most effective methods for releasing tensions that interfere with sleep is called *internal free association*. During the process of internal free association, thoughts and feelings will emerge in very strange forms and sequences. In many ways, they will be more closely related to the absurdities you often experience in dreaming than to the familiarity of logical thinking. These forms of mental expression are precisely what will relieve the id of pent up tensions.

Perhaps the best time to use this method is as you are about to fall asleep or after something has inadvertently awakened you and you are trying to get back to sleep. Any time when you can be mentally alone, however, is an appropriate time to use internal free association. You need not be physically isolated from other people. To anyone else, you will appear to be thinking quietly to yourself; no one will have any awareness of the images, feelings, and thoughts that may be coming to your awareness except you. The more often you can do internal free association, the more energies you will be diverting to your ego from the id and superego.

The method follows three very simple rules. We list them first and then go over each in more detail.

Rule 1: Do not respond to your thoughts.

Rule 2: Do not try to stop your thoughts from coming into your awareness. Let them come into your mind. Do not interfere with them.

Rule 3: Watch the thought or image as it travels through your mind and then allow it to simply float away. Do not try to rush it; let it take whatever time it needs.

Rule 1 instructs you not to respond to your thoughts. This means that when you find yourself thinking about someone or something, do not build on the thought. Do not expand it or be persuaded to interact with it. Do not answer any of its questions or try to solve any problems that may be related to it. If you sense that you are becoming involved with the thought, mentally quiet yourself with a soft and gentle "sshh." The key is to remain a passive observer.

Rule 2 asks you not to try to stop any thoughts or images from coming into your awareness. Let them come to your mind as they will. Do not interfere with their journey. Be passive. Your mind is the road that they must travel on, so let them go. For example, if an image of an associate comes to mind, don't start planning out your conversation for the next day with this person. Instead, just let the image come to your awareness. Don't do anything with it; remain passive.

Rule 3: Watch the thought or image as it travels through your mind. Look at it. Listen to it. Let it travel at its own speed and in its own direction. Don't try to control it. Don't try to change it. Then, simply allow it to float away. It will soon be replaced by another. Let it come into focus. Take a good look at it and report to yourself just what it is that you are seeing or hearing. Then, let it go.

The images will start out as orderly, predictable, and familiar. However, if you remain passive they will soon become foreign, strange, and surprising. You will find it incredible that the images and words that are passing through your mind are actually coming from you. The more passive you can remain, the less familiar will become the images.

No matter what form they may take, remain passive. Continue to follow the three rules: do not respond to them, do not interfere with them, and allow them to quietly pass into and out of your awareness. Their meaning is less important than their freedom to move through you without interference. Let them come and go.

Now, let's go through the process once again, this time with a bit more detail. Let your mind gently rest on some kind of sensation that always remains the same. For example, you may notice the continuous sound of a blower from the air-conditioning system in your office. Focus your attention on the constancy of this sensation and let your mind rest on it. Any real or imagined sensation that is constant and comfortable will work just as well. We will refer to this sensation as your "home base."

As you focus on the home base, you will soon become aware of a thought entering your mind. It will tend to disrupt your awareness of the home base. When it does, remember the three rules: do not respond to the thought or the image, do not try to stop the thought or the image, and watch the thought or the image as it comes into focus and then floats away. Simply remain passive.

Then, as the thought or the image moves away, go back to the sensation of the home base. Remember, do not respond, do not react; let it come and watch it go. As you follow these rules, something very interesting will begin to happen. You will find that your thoughts will start to change from words into images, and the images may turn into sounds. These images and sounds can take the form of just about anything. You might hear a phrase that you have never said or heard anyone else ever say. You might see the face of a stranger or even perceive a mass of colors or rotating shapes. None of the images may seem to have any logical bases of association. Any or all of them may seem very foreign as they simply pop into your awareness for no apparent reason. Whatever the image and no matter what or whom you see, the rules remain the same: do not respond, do not interfere (be passive), and watch the image as it comes into focus and then floats away. Then as it moves away, let your mind drift back to the sensations of the home base.

There is no need for you to try to analyze the images. Whatever they are, they are naturally a part of you. Despite their form, they are harmless. They are not part of reality. They are only part of your imagination. The images are enabling your ego to let go of the day's tremendous strains and pressures. Let them come and go. As you do, your ego will enable you to experience the very pleasant sensations of rest and relaxation.

This process of internal free association will discharge pent-up tensions from the id, and it will relinquish the inhibitory controls from the superego. The results will be an ego that can remain on line for longer periods of time with increased resilience to withstand the emotional pressures from the two other parts of the personality.

SUMMARY

In this chapter we have considered the concept of emotional stability in leadership. When pressures develop and conflicts arise, even the most stable of leaders is challenged to remain level headed. Decisions that are made to preserve one's personal pride or from spite or vengeance could prove disastrous to the long-term welfare of the organization.

Intelligence alone cannot assure that decisions in leadership will be made on a rational basis. However, you can use intelligence to develop and make use of the knowledge that tensions and anxieties can disable the process of rational thinking, and this can significantly contribute to emotional stability in the leadership role. Events that cause us to feel anxious and threatened were defined as superego triggers. How we deal with the superego trigger will determine the nature of our actions. If the rational dimension of our mental framework, the ego, has been operating under physical or emotional strain, it will likely collapse under the pressure of the anxieties. The id will subsequently perceive the existing anxieties as a threat to our internal balance (homeostasis) and will attempt to neutralize that threat by steering bodily energies into impulsive and aggressive behaviors. If the ego is capable of efficient operations, it can disperse the anxieties into channels of clear thinking. Actions will then be guided by the process of reason and sound judgment. The methods of time management, physical activity, and relaxation were described in this chapter as ways to increase the efficient operations of the ego.

TOPICS FOR DISCUSSION

1. Define the term emotional stability and relate it to the concepts of the id, the ego, and the superego.
2. Discuss whether or not you believe Dr. Kramer (from the case study) was an emotionally stable person. Defend your opinion based on the concepts that you learned from this chapter.
3. Define the term superego trigger and then list the types of superego triggers to which you are the most vulnerable. Include the people in your life who are most likely to "superego trigger" you.
4. Develop a plan through which you can apply the concepts of time management, physical activity, and relaxation into your daily routine. What parts of your life would have to change to accommodate this plan?

5. Apply the concepts from this chapter to a leader with whom you are familiar. Is that person emotionally stable? Why or why not? What suggestions might you offer that person if you were to be called in to provide your services as a leadership consultant?

RECOMMENDED READINGS

COOPER, K. (1977). *The aerobics way*. New York: Bantam.
GORDON, T. (1978). *Leader effectiveness training*. Solana Beach, CA.: Effectiveness Training Press.
MIRKIN, G., & HOFFMAN, M. (1978). *The sports medicine book*. Boston: Little, Brown and Company.
WEBER, R. (1980). *Time is money*. New York: The Free Press; A Division of Macmillan Publishing Company.

CHAPTER FOUR
BASIC COMMUNICATION SKILLS

OUTLINE

MAJOR CONCERNS
INTRODUCTION
BASIC COMMUNICATION SKILLS

   Conversation
   Assertiveness
   Confrontation
   Feedback
   Dealing with Criticism

SUMMARY
TOPICS FOR DISCUSSION
RECOMMENDED READINGS

MAJOR CONCEPTS

1. A *superego desensitizer* can be defined as any behavior (gesture or comment) that reduces anxiety. This reduction of anxiety signals the ego that the external environment does not pose a threat to the body's internal balance.
2. An extremely effective way to begin a conversation is to stimulate the other person to talk about him- or herself.
3. Assertiveness should be distinguished from aggression. *Aggressive behavior* seeks self-satisfaction without regard for the other person's welfare. It is usually driven by force and is controlled by impulsive power. *Assertive behavior* likewise seeks self-satisfaction. However, it usually accomplishes results without jeopardizing the welfare of other people.
4. When workers do deviate from the leader's expectations, their actions must be *confronted, understood,* and *modified* according to the leader's discretion and prudent judgment.
5. The basic procedures for giving criticism involve *preparation, confrontation, response, feedback,* and *closure.*
6. For a confrontation to achieve its desired effect, it must minimize the risks of triggering the subordinate's superego.
7. The overall effect of confrontive and constructive criticism is that these criticisms force a person *to think* (ego), rather than allow a person *to react* impulsively (id).
8. The use of *silence* on the leader's part can be an effective tool for keeping the conversation focused on the subordinate's concerns.
9. *Reflective listening* is a potent tool for establishing that both parties have understood one another before finishing a conversation.
10. To listen effectively, you must tune out distractions.
11. When you are on the receiving end of the criticism, your own ego should enable you to hear the facts behind the subordinate's criticism of you.

INTRODUCTION

In Chapter 3 we discussed the concept of emotional stability as a necessary component of effective leadership. The threat to that stability was identified as the superego trigger. In this chapter, we will be concentrating on how a leader can prevent the effects of superego triggers from compromising the productive functions of the work team.

The chapter will focus on a set of basic communication skills. These skills will each revolve around a concept called the *superego desensitizer*. A superego desensitizer can be defined as any behavior (gesture or comment) that reduces anxiety. This reduction of anxiety signals the ego that the external environment does not pose a threat to the body's internal balance. Since the id has no need to relieve pain, it does not drain energy from the cortex. Consequently, energy levels remain sufficient to sustain ego operations. Unlike the superego trigger, the superego desensitizer calms the superego and in effect signals the id that the threat to homeostasis has been neutralized. As a result, the id has no reason to launch impulsive behavior since there is no anxiety to relieve.

BASIC COMMUNICATION SKILLS

Conversation

The earliest stages of developing relationships involve getting to know one another. For some people, conversation comes very naturally. However, a great many people have difficulty making conversation. Research in an area of social science called *pragmatics* has established that conversations typically follow a predictable and consistent format (Wilcox, 1983).

1. Conversational initiation:
   a. The willingness to initiate a conversation
   b. The ability to initiate a conversation
   c. The outcome of the initiation strategies
2. Conversational maintenance:
   a. Strategies for maintaining the conversation
   b. Strategies for maintaining a particular topic
3. Turn taking:
   a. The willingness to shift listener-speaker roles
   b. The realization as to when role shifting is needed
   c. Strategies for shifting roles
4. Conversational repair:
   a. Recognition of conversation breakdown
   b. Strategies for repairing the conversational flow
5. Termination:
   a. Strategies for terminating the topic
   b. Strategies for terminating the conversation

An extremely effective way to begin a conversation is to make it easy for other people to talk about themselves. Remember that the id is totally self-centered. When you allow attention to focus on the other person, the id is able to discharge its energies in a nondestructive and self-gratifying manner. This principle is precisely why people enjoy talking about themselves in preference to almost any other subject. An emotional bond usually develops for two reasons. First, you allow the other person to talk about whatever she considers to be important—an opportunity which is very rare indeed. It feels good. As a result, she associates you with positive feelings. Second, even though her topic focuses on herself, her attention is directed toward you. She will want to say things that will sustain your attention.

What you say in attempt to engage another person in a conversation is less important than the amount of interest you convey in making contact. The more interest that you show, the more willing the other person will be to talk with you. You can get him to talk about himself through a *direct* or *indirect approach.*

The direct approach involves the use of standard opening statements followed by inquiries about the other person. The standard openers are, of course, expressions such as "Hello," "How are you?" "What's your name?" "Where are you from?", and so forth. Once you have established contact with the other person, you can begin the process of direct inquiry. Be alert to any cues you might pick up from the way the person was introduced to you. Then inquire about these cues. The inquiries might include asking about any or all of the following topics:

1. Line of work:
   a. How they chose it
   b. Specifics about training for it (when, where, etc.)
   c. Particular areas of interest related to it
   d. Changes they would make in it if they could
2. Family:
   a. Size
   b. Location
   c. Birth order
   d. Stories about spouse, children, parents, siblings
3. Incidental comments relating to:
   a. Manner of dress
   b. Manner of speech (accents, dialects)
   c. Hobbies
   d. Special interests

e. Political beliefs
f. Most embarrassing moments
g. Things that make them angry
h. Secrets to their success (dieting, quitting smoking)

One indirect approach for getting a person to talk about him- or herself involves starting a conversation by focusing on a situation that the two of you have in common. You may find yourself standing next to the person waiting for a elevator that always seems to be unbearably slow. Talk about it. You may have overheard the person stating that she had seen a movie you particularly liked or disliked. Bring it up. You may have seen the person shopping at one of your favorite or least favorite stores. Discuss it. By using the situation that you have both experienced, you are establishing that the two of you share something in common. Once other people begin talking in response to your introductory comments, you can start to focus the conversation on their interests. They will then naturally slip into talking about themselves.

A second type of indirect approach for getting a person to talk about himself involves starting a conversation by initially focusing the topic on yourself. You might nonchalantly start talking about any of the above situations as they relate to your own feelings, interests, predicaments, or beliefs. In many cases, something you say will trigger a response from the other person relating to something that happened to him. At that point, he will likely begin talking about himself.

Assertiveness

To successfully direct human resources a leader should ideally state objectives, give directions, and announce policies in a manner that does not trigger defensive behaviors. The members of the work team require clear and specific information from the person in charge. Forceful direction by a leader is, in effect, a superego trigger that floods the subordinate's ego with anxiety. Since the majority of subordinates lack insight about human temperament, it is safe to assume that a subordinate's ego would be relatively unable to cope with superego anxiety in a reasonable manner. The anxiety represents a threat to homeostasis. The id diverts energy from the cortex which causes the ego to function inefficiently. The id then generates impulsive actions to relieve the distress—actions that are usually counterproductive to the leader's efforts.

Aggressive forms of leadership can produce conformity among subordinates. However, a great deal of research has documented that aggression does not foster productivity. It may certainly intimidate workers into completing their work tasks. However, it fails to motivate them or generate within them a sense of company belonging; it fails to foster loyalty to the company or contribute creatively to the company's development. The ability for a business to survive appears to be related to the extent it respects the personal needs of its employees. This consideration translates to flexibility in leadership and to interpersonal sensitivity in personnel policies.

Assertiveness should be distinguished from aggression. *Aggressive behavior* seeks self-satisfaction without regard for the other person's welfare. It is usually driven by force and is controlled by impulsive power. *Assertive behavior* likewise seeks self-satisfaction. However, it usually accomplishes results without jeopardizing the welfare of other people.

Assertive statements are directed by the ego. That is, they are judiciously controlled having been prepared with forethought and consideration. By using assertive statements to define expectations and to clarify job functions, leaders address the egos of their subordinates. The risk of triggering superego defenses and impulsive reactions are drastically minimized as compared with aggressive expressions. In defining expectations and clarifying the roles of subordinates, it is imperative for the leader to make his or her wants and needs clear without intentionally jeopardizing the needs of others. The use of assertive statements informs rather than intimidates.

Examples include statements such as:

I want . . .
I expect . . .
The tasks in your job specifically include . . .
The time to submit your report is . . .
The person to whom you are responsible is . . .

Assertive statements may also be used to correct, to refuse, to teach, to express opinions, to express appreciation, and to offer criticism as in the following examples:

No, that is not the correct procedure. Here is the sequence I want you to follow.
No, I will not be available to participate in that project.

I want you to learn these principles by applying them in the meeting tomorrow.

I disagree with that interpretation. The amount budgeted is insufficient because . . .

I appreciate the support you gave me in completing the report. It saved me a great deal of time.

Your comments assisted me in understanding the concept of aerodynamics. At the same time, I would have found them more useful if you had incorporated an example to illustrate each point.

Note that each of the comments expresses your thoughts directly. There are no apologies or softening statements such as:

I probably am not qualified to say this, but . . .
Do you really think that is such a good idea?

Once ideas and expectations have been expressed, the leader should be prepared to handle the subordinate's reactions in a manner that is equally judicious. Remember, in principle find responses that incorporate superego desensitizers rather than superego triggers.

In general, the following steps should serve as a useful guideline:

1. Stop to listen.
2. Be patient.
3. Be reasonable.
4. Be understanding.
5. Be tactful.

Through this process of assertive statement followed by efforts to understand, you and the subordinates will be able to agree upon roles that are consistent with your responsibilities in leadership and that are supportive of the subordinate's personal and professional needs.

Confrontation

When workers do deviate from the leader's expectations, their actions must be confronted, understood, and modified according to the leader's discretion and prudent judgment. The delivery of criticism is, therefore, a necessary component of leadership. Giving criticism can never be construed as a pleasant task. Under the best of circumstances, the person receiving the criticism will experience at least some degree of tension and anxiety. Nonetheless, the leader's role, after having accessed his or her own ego, is to express the criticism by consciously attempting to avoid the use of superego triggers. The object is to deliver information that will change the subordinate's work performance without jeopardizing the working relationship.

The basic procedures for giving criticism involve preparation, confrontation, response, feedback, and closure (Bach & Goldberg, 1975). Each of these procedures will be described. Specific guidelines for the entire set of procedures will then be listed.

The preparation phase actually includes self-preparation and preparing the subordinate for the confrontation. Gain composure, think rationally, and maintain adequate levels of patience and stability. Think clearly about what behavior you want the subordinate to change. Select the time, place, and choice of words by which the confrontation will occur.

It is extremely important that the subordinate not be caught off-guard. Otherwise, the unexpected confrontation would significantly trigger the subordinate's superego, which would, in turn, release tremendous levels of anxiety. To avoid this source of unnecessary tension, simply approach the subordinate during a relatively low-stress period. Mention that you would like to meet at a time that is mutually convenient to discuss the issue in question. Usually, if you encourage him to pull out his calendar while you have yours in hand, you will be refocusing the attention from the area of sensitivity to that of scheduling. This refocusing tends to reduce anxiety and helps to access the subordinate's ego, at least momentarily.

In addition to setting a specific time and place, agree on the extent of time that you would like to devote to the discussion. Once again, pinpointing these details removes some of the uncertainty and, therefore, helps to reduce the levels of anxiety. As the anxiety is reduced, so too is the subordinate's need for defensive maneuvers. Be calm, low key, move slowly, react patiently, and simply work toward agreeing on where you will meet, when, and for how long. In spite of the fact that you will need to confront the person's inappropriate behavior, superego desensitizers will be one of your most powerful tools for bringing the behaviors back in line with the company's requirements.

The confrontation phase of giving criticism is the time during which you actually state your concerns, objections, and instructions for behavioral change. It is extremely important for you to keep your comments focused on the subordinate's unacceptable behavior, not on the subordinate's personality. Remember, if you trigger his superego, it will be natural for him to resist you with overt or passive aggression.

Just prior to confronting the subordinate, restate the purpose of the meeting and indicate your hope that the two of you can work together to understand and resolve the issues that have caused the difficulties.

For a confrontation to achieve its desired effect, it must minimize the risks of triggering the subordinate's superego. Drs. George Bach and Herb Goldberg describe such a confrontation as a "Statement of the Beef and Its Hurtful Impact." In describing the situation between a comptroller in a manufacturing firm and the firm's personnel manager, they provided the following example (Bach & Goldberg, 1975):

> COMPTROLLER: You hired Mr. McDonald to computerize our payroll system . . . You didn't ask if he was acceptable to me nor whether I felt he had the necessary background to do this job. It makes me feel pressured and overloaded, as I'm the one who's ultimately responsible.

A useful form in which to phrase a confrontation consists of three categories: first, a reference to the behavior in nonblameful terms; second, a remark that indicates how the behavior created a problem for the leader; and third, a statement that reflects the leader's emotional reactions to the behavior (Gordon, 1978). Looking at the preceding example, we can see that the statements indeed fit within the three categories:

> *Behavioral reference*: You hired Mr. McDonald to computerize our payroll system . . . . You didn't ask if he was acceptable to me nor whether I felt he had the necessary background to do the job.
> *Problem reference*: I'm the one who is ultimately responsible.
> *Feeling reference*: It makes me feel pressured and overloaded.

The very process of thinking about criticism in these terms requires the leader to operate within his or her ego. Sorting thoughts into specific divisions requires a special kind of analysis. Accordingly, this process delays impulses from being acted out. Instead, the ego diverts the impulses into feelings that can be expressed in terms of the emotional effects of the subordinate's actions on the leader. For example, by stating, "It makes me feel pressured and overloaded," you enable the id to harmlessly discharge superego anxieties through a set of words that communicate your experiences rather than ridicule the subordinate.

In addition to confrontation, *constructive criticism* is another format for giving criticism that is highly appropriate when your opinion is either requested or necessitated. Suppose, for example, that you have asked a subordinate to prepare a report. In reviewing the results, you determine that a number of changes are needed to bring the report up to standard. Depending upon your own time constraints and related pressures, your comments might trigger the subordinate's superego and cause her to flare up against you and subsequently resist your directions. An alternative that will more than likely communicate your reactions is the use of superego desensitizers combined with directions for making specific modifications. This format involves two types of statements. First, let the subordinate know what you found useful about her report:

I was interested in the way you expressed . . .
The way you described . . . is effective because . . .
It was useful for me to read your comments about . . . because . . .

Second, advise the subordinate as to alternative forms of expressions within the report that would alleviate the concerns you have about specific points:

It would have been more useful to me if you would have phrased paragraph two in this way because . . .
I was confused when I read this section. It would make more sense to me if you would change it to read . . .
A form that I am more experienced with is . . . and I would like you to reframe the report in the same way. Then, let's take another look at it.

The overall effect of confrontive and constructive criticism is that these types of criticism force you to think (ego), rather than allow you to impulsively react (id). The result is that you have confronted the subordinate with her unacceptable behavior in a way that has accessed your ego. You are now ready to deal with the subordinate's reaction in a judicious manner. Your ego is on line.

Once you have stated the criticism, the next phase is to allow the subordinate *an opportunity to respond*. Despite the amount of care you have taken to assure that the subordinate will not feel attacked, to some extent, she probably will. Confrontation, in just about any form, makes people anxious. Of course, the way in which you prepared the other person for the confrontation as well as the nonblameful wording you employed will trigger far less tension and anxiety than if your comments had been impulsively based. Nonetheless, expect some degree of defensiveness. Your confrontation, though targeted for her ego, will be received by her superego which will trigger anxiety.

The next step is to let the subordinate respond. The response will more than likely be coming from her id. Remember, the id's job is to relieve pain. The most typical way to accomplish this relief is through a counterattack. So, the subordinate, in one form or another, will probably snap back at you; it may be through her tone of voice, her silence, hostile words, or any combination thereof. By understanding the reasons underlying the subordinate's reactions, you will be using your own ego to help the subordinate lower her levels of anxiety. The very process of letting her talk without interruption will help her ventilate a great deal of tension.

The third step is to help the subordinate to continue talking for awhile. Remember that people seldom have the opportunity to talk about themselves. Most of the time, other people cut them off. By allowing and actively enabling the subordinate to talk about her anger, frustration, humiliation, or whatever other reactions she may have experienced as a result of your confrontation, you are again making it possible for her id to discharge tension in a nondestructive way. The two ways to keep her talking are to simply not interrupt her and to use door openers (Gordon, 1978).

Interruptions are so common that oftentimes they go unnoticed. In a heated situation, however, people become highly sensitized whenever an interruption breaks into their attempts to have their say. Resist your temptation to interrupt. Let the subordinate finish his phrases, his sentences, his entire chain of thought. The use of silence on your part can be an effective tool for keeping the conversation focused on the subordinate's concerns. Remain quiet for a time after he has stopped talking. Give him a chance to rethink what he has just said. This quiet period will also help to calm him down. This is a time when you need to be as still, relaxed, slow moving, and quiet as you possibly can. Your confrontation will have agitated him. Now, your job is to help him take in what you have said and adjust to it. Work to bring down his anxiety by supporting his own efforts to do so.

In addition to making use of quiet time to encourage the subordinate to ventilate, the use of door openers will help him continue to talk with you. The door opener is an open-ended question that invites the speaker to tell you more about something he has only briefly mentioned. You can pick up on a word, phrase, or concept that he expressed and then repeat it to him with a questioning tone in your voice that suggests you would like him to talk some more about it. You can also express a bit of confusion over something he said and inquire further about it. For example, "I guess I was confused when you mentioned the unfair salary policies. Can you help me understand?" In general, as long as you can help the subordinate use words to ventilate his tensions, the levels of his anxiety will come down. His id will discover that the danger is subsiding. Energies will be rechanneled to his ego. He will be in a better position to hear the facts behind your concerns (Benjamin, 1969).

Feedback

The next procedure in the confrontation cycle is to *feedback the information* that the subordinate has expressed to you. Your feedback is a way of communicating that his or her reaction has made an impact on you in a way that you can handle. The feedback demonstrates that you have understood his or her concerns and that it is entirely possible that two people can reasonably discuss a sensitive issue.

Refelective listening is a potent tool for establishing that both parties have understood one another before finishing a conversation. People seldom leave conversations with any assurance that their listener has really understood what it was they were trying to express. Verbal communication is highly sensitive to misunderstanding. For example, consider the sentence:

"My manager said he would tell us who gets laid off next week."

A listener might conclude that the speaker could lose his job *next week*. The speaker might have meant that *next week* his manager would announce *future* layoffs. Many conflicts have ensued because of misunderstandings that could be traced to miscommunications. People often hear what they want or perhaps dread to hear. Oftentimes, the intended meaning is just the opposite.

The process of reflective listening significantly reduces the risks that such misunderstandings will occur. In reflective listening, the listener feeds the message back to the speaker in the listener's own words. The form is usually a brief summary of the expression. If the summary is consistent with the speaker's intended message, the speaker will typically respond with a verbal confirmation such as "right." If the summary is inconsistent, the speaker will typically correct the listener and thereby resolve the ambiguity. To return to the sentence above, the listener's response might have been:

"If I'm understanding you correctly, you're worried that you might lose your job next week."

The speaker would likely reply:

"No, its not me that I'm worried about. My job, as far as I know, is secure. No, once my manager makes the announcements next week, I'm going to have to tell several of my subordinates that they have 30 days to find another job."

To listen effectively, you must tune out distractions. Concentrate on the message that the person is trying to convey. One author expressed this concept in terms of listening with the third ear (Reik, 1948). You are attempting to truly understand what the speaker is experiencing as he is expressing his thoughts to you. This process is never an easy one, even for the most experienced of listeners.

As you summarize your understanding of what the speaker has said to you, remain calm, slow moving, and relaxed. Your interest is simply to establish that you have indeed realized the importance of the subordinate's concerns and that before you comment further on them, you can see the logic and reasoning that underlies his thinking. In other words, not only does the feedback verify that you did understand his thoughts, it also further desensitizes his superego, calms his id, and facilitates the on-line operations of his ego.

Feedback consists of summarizing the content of the speaker's expression in a manner that is comfortable and natural for you. Many courses that teach the concept of "active listening" include practice drills in which students are taught to use such phrases as:

Sounds like what you are saying is . .
You feel that . . .

Phrases such as these quickly become overused and make both the active listener and the other person feel unnatural and uncomfortable. The easiest and most genuine way to give feedback is to simply find out if you really have understood what the other person said. Make sure you do not use the same phrasing over and again. Avoid using words or styles that will suggest that you are not being yourself. Use an *occasional* statement such as, "Let me make sure I'm with you so far." Then, go on to summarize as in the following examples:

You don't think I've been fair in assigning you to the project because . . .
What worries you about the meeting tomorrow is . . .
The way you see the problem is that . . .

Remember, avoid using the same introductory statements more than just a few times with the same person. Even at that, spread them out so that you are not saying the same thing in succession. There are countless ways to make statements of feedback. Taking the time to come up with your own puts you squarely in your ego. At that point, you will be better able to put yourself across in a low-key, patient, and prudent manner.

The target response that you are working towards in giving feedback is a confirmation from the subordinate that you have understood correctly. The usual response is "right." This kind of response (others may include "yes," "that's it," "exactly") indicates that you have understood the content of the subordinate's expression. Her tone of voice will confirm that you have understood her feelings as well. The tone can vary, of course. However, you will clearly recognize that the defensiveness is subsiding. Her rate of speech will slow down, and her voice will become softer and lower in pitch. These changes will be your indication that her anxiety level will have come down and that she is making the transition from her id to her ego. It is at this point where decisions can be made regarding the need for changes in the subordinate's work performance.

The closing phase is the period during which you need to reconfront the subordinate to make the change in the behaviors that were unacceptable to you. By this point, the subordinate should be much more receptive to your concerns since he no longer has strong needs to defend himself. As before, state the specific behavior that has caused you a problem, indicate how the behavior has created difficulties for you, and make him aware of how you feel as a result. In addition, call for the changes that you expect the subordinate to make in order to correct the current problem and to prevent the problem from recurring. Be prepared to let the subordinate respond to the confrontation, to listen to his concerns, and to verify that you have understood his position. Close the meeting by asking the subordinate to summarize his understanding of your expectations and to indicate whether or not he is willing to conform with the conditions that you have discussed. Make sure that you stay within the time limits that you established for this meeting. Should you notice that your time will not be sufficient to accomplish your objective, stop the discussion at least 5 minutes prior to the time limit. Then, refocus the discussion on scheduling another meeting so that neither of you will feel pressured into agreeing to terms that you might later regret.

In many cases, this process will be sufficient to help the subordinate make the changes in accordance with your directions and specifications. The objective is to work with the subordinate to activate his ego. The rationale that underlies the objective is that his inappropriate work performance was related to either a misunderstanding of your expectations, a defensive maneuver to maintain his own dignity, or both. The intervention strategy has been to state the facts, use superego desensitizers to help him hear the facts, and then to restate the facts once his ego has been accessed.

The process of giving criticism within a constructive framework has been described as consisting of four phases: preparation, confrontation, feedback, and closure. The procedural guidelines for these phases are as follows:

Procedural Guidelines for
Constructive and Confrontive Criticism

THE PREPARATION PHASE

1. Access your ego.
2. Approach the subordinate during a relatively low-stress period.
3. Indicate that you would like to meet at a time that is mutually convenient to discuss an issue that has been concerning you.
4. Identify the issue.
5. State how much time is needed to discuss the issue in more detail.
6. If the present time is not suitable for one or both of you, refocus the conversation from the specific issue to scheduling a specific meeting time.
7. Summarize the arrangements to verify that you are both in agreement.

THE CONFRONTATION PHASE—
CONFRONTIVE CRITICISM

1. Access your own ego.
2. Restate the purpose of the meeting.
3. Express your hope that the two of you can work together to understand and resolve the issues that have caused the difficulties.
4. Help the subordinate get physically comfortable in the setting. Offer coffee, a soft drink, or whatever else might help to place you and the subordinate at greater ease.
5. Focus your confrontive comments on the unacceptable behavior, not on the personality characteristics of the subordinate.
6. Indicate how the subordinate's actions have interfered with your own work performance. Specific reference may be made to costs in time, energy, money, safety, or security.
7. Reflect your feelings about these costs in terms of anger, frustration, resentment, confusion, worry, and so forth.

THE CONFRONTATION PHASE—
CONSTRUCTIVE CRITICISM

1. See steps 1–4 under Confrontive Criticism.

2. Focus first on the ways in which the subordinate's work met with your expectations and helped the work team to accomplish the objectives.
3. Make a transition from the utility of the work performance to the ways in which the items about the work should be changed to make a more effective contribution.

THE RESPONSE PHASE

1. Let the subordinate respond to the confrontation.
2. Do not interrupt the subordinate.
    a. Remain quiet.
    b. Use appropriate gestures and vocal affirmations to acknowledge that you want the subordinate to continue.
3. Use open-ended questions to help the subordinate keep talking.

THE FEEDBACK PHASE

1. Periodically feed back the points that the subordinate has expressed to you.
2. Avoid relying on the same phrasing over and over again, and do not use trite or hackneyed expressions.
3. Use your own style so that you can feel and sound like yourself.
4. Remain calm, slow moving, low key, and relaxed.
5. Work towards target response from the subordinate such as "right," "yes," that's it," "uh-huh," etc.
6. Summarize the major issues to make sure that you have understood the subordinate's point of view.

THE CLOSING PHASE

1. State the specific behavior that has caused you a problem, indicate what the problems were, and express your feelings that you experienced in reaction to them.
2. Call for the changes that you expect the subordinate to make in order to correct the current problem and in order to prevent the problem from recurring.
3. Be prepared to let the subordinate respond to the confrontation, to listen to the subordinate's concerns, and to verify that you have understood his or her position.
4. Close the meeting by asking the subordinate to summarize his or her understanding of your expectations and to indicate whether or not the subordinate is willing to conform to the conditions that you have outlined.

5. If the subordinate is unwilling or hesitant to meet your expectations, move to the Procedural Guidelines for Problem Solving. (See ch. 5)
6. Stay within the time limits you established for this meeting.
7. Schedule another meeting as needed to make sure that neither of you feel pressured into agreeing to terms that you might later regret.

Dealing with Criticism

In the previous sections, you learned how to direct criticism toward the subordinate's ego. When you are on the receiving end of the criticism, your own ego should enable you to hear the facts behind the subordinate's criticism of you. Once you can access your ego, you will have reduced your vulnerability to superego triggers through which subordinate's may try to attack you.

The principle for dealing with criticism is to regard the criticism as an expression from the subordinate's id. You have already learned how to handle outbursts from another person's id. Since the id's job is to relieve pain through impulsive rather than rational action, your job is to soothe the id so that the pain can be relieved nondestructively. In other words, by using superego desensitizers, you will diminish the subordinate's anxiety. As the anxiety level comes down, the id will begin to release its grip on the subordinate's actions, energy will return to the ego, and rational thinking will start to occur.

The steps to use are identical to the *response* and *feedback* phases that were discussed with regard to giving criticism. First, let the subordinate have her say. Do not interrupt her. Show an interest in what she has to say. Try to determine the facts and reasons behind the emotions. Get in touch with the emotions that are fueling her expressions. Your objective at this point is to make it easy for her to tell you what she wants you to know. If you resist, argue, shut her off, or try to overpower her, you will trigger her superego to flood her ego with anxiety. Her ego will more than likely go off line, her id will take over, and her criticism will become more intense and increasingly impulsive. Your first superego desensitizer, therefore, will be to give her a chance to talk to you. Remain quiet, keep your movements slow and relaxed, and acknowledge her statements with head nods.

Use door openers and feedback to keep her talking and to verify that you have understood what she wants you to know. Summarize her main points and ask her if you have understood her correctly. Following your summary, see if there is anything she would like to add that she has not yet brought up. This is the time for her to get everything out in the open that she may have been bottling up.

Remember, it is very seldom that people get to ventilate in this way. As you allow the subordinate to go through this experience, she will begin to calm down, feel less like fighting you, and more and more like allowing you to help her. Dealing with criticism in this way provides an opportunity to convert a problem employee into one of the most loyal members of the work team.

Once criticism has been fully expressed, you can evaluate how a particular worker's needs can be addressed in a way that will not compromise the company's welfare. Ask her what she would like you to do. Get as many details as possible in terms of the specific resources you will need to make available to resolve her concerns. The end result will be to make whatever changes that you can to resolve the worker's concerns without jeopardizing the company's objectives, without creating problems for other members of the work team, or without interference to your own responsibilities.

Procedural Guidelines for Dealing with Criticism

1. Let the subordinate state the criticism.
2. Do not interrupt.
3. Show an interest in what the subordinate tells you.
4. Try to determine the facts and figures behind the emotions that are expressed.
5. Make it easy for the subordinate to say what he or she wants you to know.
6. Keep your movements slow and relaxed.
7. Use door openers and feedback to keep the subordinate talking and to verify that you have understood what he or she wants you to know.
8. Ask the subordinate what he or she would like you to do.
9. Summarize the main points, ask if you have understood correctly, and give an opportunity to add anything else that the subordinate would like you to consider.
10. Make whatever changes that you can to resolve the subordinate's concerns without jeopardizing any of the company's resources.

SUMMARY

In this chapter we have focused on basic communication skills that can be used by a leader to develop and maintain productive relations among members of the work team. The skills revolve around the concept of the superego desensitizer. The superego desensitizer helps to reduce anxiety so that behaviors are determined by the reasoning capacities of the ego rather than the impulsive mechanisms of the id. The specific skills that were discussed included conversation, assertiveness, confrontation, feedback, and dealing with criticism.

TOPICS FOR DISCUSSION

1. Differentiate between superego triggers and superego desensitizers.
2. What are some topics a person might raise in order to make it easy for you to talk about yourself?
3. Think of a person who has helped you through some difficult times. What have they said or done that made you feel comfortable and made it easy for you to say whatever was on your mind?
4. Differentiate between the concepts of aggressive, assertive, and nonassertive types of behavior. Relate these concepts to the id, ego, and superego.

RECOMMENDED READINGS

BACH, G., & GOLDBERG, H. (1975). *Creative aggression—The art of assertive living.* New York: Avon.

BENJAMIN, A. (1969). *The helping interview.* Boston: Houghton Mifflin Company.

LIKERT, R., & LIKERT, J. (1976). *New ways of managing conflict.* New York: McGraw-Hill.

REIK, T. (1948). *Listening with the third ear.* San Diego, Ca.: Harcourt Brace Jovanovich.

RUSHER, W. (1981). *How to win arguments more often than not.* New York: Doubleday.

WELLS, T. (1980). *How to keep your cool under fire—communicating nondefensively.* New York: McGraw-Hill.

CHAPTER FIVE
APPLIED COMMUNICATION: DIRECTIONS AND POLICIES

OUTLINE

MAJOR CONCEPTS
INTRODUCTION
SETTING THE AGENDA

>The Formal Agenda
>The Informal Agenda

SPEAKING BEFORE A GROUP
GIVING DIRECTIONS
ANNOUNCING POLICIES
MANAGING INTERRUPTIONS
DECISION MAKING

>Arbitration
>Team Decision Making

CONSEQUENCES FOR UNSATISFACTORY PERFORMANCE
SUMMARY
TOPICS FOR DISCUSSION
RECOMMENDED READINGS

MAJOR CONCEPTS

1. An *agenda* is a format that prepares participants for events in which they will be involved.

2. The agenda should be sent to the participants at least a day in advance of the meeting. It is also helpful if the agenda is displayed during the meeting itself.

3. The counterpart of the agenda is the set of notes that are recorded to summarize the business transacted during the meeting.

4. The format of an informal agenda will likely be verbal rather than written down as a document. The primary purpose of the informal agenda is to establish the objective to be accomplished as a result of the meeting.

5. A carefully planned agenda will help to access the ego of each participant so as to foster participation and cooperation and to minimize behaviors that are defensive, aggressive, and self-serving.

6. Your success in projecting an image of leadership and in becoming recognized as a representative of your organization will depend in large part on your competence in speaking.

7. There are four basic steps to follow when you want a group of people to recognize you as an authority on the podium. First, get their attention. Second, spell out your objectives. Third, tell them what you expect them to do to accomplish your objectives. Finally, let them know what success or failure at accomplishing your objectives will mean to them.

8. The members of the work team require clear and specific directions from the person in charge.

9. The leader should present the directions through the use of brief, direct, and action-oriented sentences.

10. The leader should not only convey that he is decisive, but equally important, that he regards the members of the work team with dignity and respect.

11. Inform the work team of the *creation, revision,* and *termination* of policies that either directly or indirectly affect the work team.

12. Retain your control of the power to lead at all times. If your subordinates are allowed to take power away from you, your ability to maintain your authority will have been compromised. Interruptions represent one means by which you could very easily lose your control.

13. The most effective way to deal with an interruption is to identify it at the very instant it occurs. To allow an interruption to continue,

whether intentionally or by default, risks the prospect of a snow-ball effect in which the original interruption could spawn chain reactions from other members, all attempting to have their own say in their own defense.

14. Two ways by which the leader can attempt to restore stability are through arbitration and team problem solving.

15. *Arbitration* is a form of problem solving in which the leader arrives at unilateral decisions after weighing evidence from all parties involved.

16. *Team problem solving* is a process that incorporates the participation of everyone involved in the dispute.

17. A business cannot succeed if its workers drain rather than contribute to its resources. As such, advising the subordinate of the consequences for unsatisfactory performance paints a picture of the reality that both the leader and the subordinate must face.

INTRODUCTION

In Chapter 4 we considered skills that can be used to establish and maintain interpersonal communication within an organization. In this chapter, we will build on those skills and apply them so that you can give direction to the flow of work in the organization. The skills revolve around the definition of leadership presented in Chapter 1. Recall that a leader is an individual who has the authority to decide, direct, and represent the objectives and functions of an organization. As such, you will become acquainted with procedures that will help you set an agenda, develop platform skills, take charge of a group, give directions, announce policies, make decisions, and administer consequences for unsatisfactory performance.

SETTING THE AGENDA

An agenda is a format that prepares participants for events in which they will be involved. The preparation accesses their ego in that it enables them to think about the events that will take place. Since an agenda structures the activities, the participant knows what will occur, in what sequence, and over a specific period of time. The agenda indicates that the meeting will have order and will, therefore, be somewhat predictable. In short, the agenda reduces levels of potential anxiety since it removes elements of the unknown from consideration. Two types of agendas involve formats for formal and informal meetings.

The Formal Agenda

The formal agenda is used for two main purposes. One purpose is to advise participants about the details of an upcoming meeting. The agenda would include the time, date, and location of the meeting. In addition, agenda items for discussion and resolution would be listed in chronological sequence. For example, items of "old business" would be listed before items of "new business."

A second purpose is to enable participants to add items to the agenda if such participation is appropriate. This form of participation offers workers an invitation and an opportunity to influence, if not decide, the policies which govern their actions.

The agenda should be sent to the participants at least a day in advance of the meeting. It is also helpful if the agenda is displayed during the meeting itself. The display will help you as the leader to keep the participants task-oriented. It will serve as documentation of the meeting's objectives for when discussions tend to go off on tangents as they so often do.

The counterpart of the agenda is the set of notes that are recorded to summarize the business transacted during the meeting. These notes are generally referred to as the *minutes*. The minutes typically parallel the agenda items, unless the order of business followed a different course. Minutes can vary in detail, though accuracy should never be compromised. The most vital information for recording includes the item up for discussion, the rationale for its inclusion, the discussion of its pros and cons, and the decision regarding its implementation. In some cases, a simple entry regarding an announcement to inform the participants of some mattter will be sufficient. However, the carefully planned agenda will include a specific time for announcements. Accordingly, the minutes will reflect such entries as announcements in their proper order. Minutes will also report the names of participants in attendance, the date, place, and beginning-ending times of the meeting. The recorder will generally sign the minutes. The leader should review, edit, and correct the minutes for accuracy and style immediately after a rough draft has been prepared. The recorder should distribute a finished, typed draft of the minutes during the next working day following the meeting. The minutes should be distributed to all individuals who are responsible or accountable for the information that was exchanged during the meeting whether or not they had been in attendance. The formal approval of the minutes should be the first item of business on the agenda for the next meeting.

Long-term records of the minutes should be maintained and cataloged. Since as a leader you are accountable for the actions of your work team, you must have access to these minutes on a moment's notice. Your storage systems should provide for both chronological and categorical retrieval. In other words, if you need information regarding announcements of productivity during the previous fiscal year, you can retrieve the items by day, month, and year and by the categories of productivity or by announcements. There are currently many sources of software available for microcomputers that provide filing system capabilities. The storage of minutes is an excellent application.

Procedural Guidelines for the Formal Agenda

1. Use the agenda to advise participants about the details of the upcoming meeting.
2. If appropriate, allow the participants to request their own items for consideration on the agenda.
3. List the date, place, and beginning-ending times of the meeting.
4. List the items in chronological sequence that parallels the intended progression for their discussion.
5. Provide each participant or otherwise accountable individual with a copy of the agenda at least one day in advance of the meeting.
6. Display the agenda prominently during the meeting.
7. Record the transactions of the meeting in a set of minutes.
8. The recording of the minutes should parallel the format of the agenda.
9. The minutes should never compromise accuracy, though detail of recording may vary with the leader's individual preference.
10. Standard items of entry within the minutes should include the names of those present and absent, the date, the location, and the beginning-ending times.
11. The recorder should sign the minutes.
12. The leader should review, edit, and approve the minutes regarding accuracy of content and style.
13. The recorder should distribute the minutes during the next working day following the meeting.
14. Formal approval of the minutes should be entered as the first item for activity on the agenda for the next meeting.
15. Long-term records of the agendas and their corresponding minutes should be maintained for storage and retrieval.

The Informal Agenda

Whenever a leader schedules a meeting that directly involves or at least impacts members of the work team, a formal agenda should be prepared. There are times when the leader requests to have a meeting with specific members of the work team or honors requests by such members to hold a meeting. The content of the meeting will pertain to the needs of those specific members rather than to the needs of the group at large. In such cases, a formal agenda is not required.

The informal agenda will serve many of the same purposes in the individualized meetings as the formal agenda served for the larger group. However, the format of an informal agenda will likely be verbal rather than written down as a document. The primary purpose of the informal agenda is to establish the objective to be accomplished as a result of the meeting. If two people agree to meet, it is vital that both approach the meeting with the same understanding of what it is they are both attempting to accomplish. Serious problems may develop if the individuals come to the meeting with differing assumptions as to its purpose. The informal agenda, first and foremost, establishes the reason that the meeting will occur. This type of agenda also specifies the times, date, and location for the meeting. In addition, it can establish the tone by which the meeting will be conducted. For example, the agenda might indicate that the participants will relax over coffee or, by contrast, that the meeting will take place in the offices of the corporate attorney.

In any event, the agenda prepares each of the participants for the meeting by specifying details about scheduling, content, and objectives. The informality of the agenda relates to the verbal delivery rather than a written document. It establishes that each of the participants agree to attend the meeting, the details of scheduling and location, and the purpose for which the meeting is being called. An informal agenda might be delivered in the following way:

> "John, I'd like us to discuss the cost overruns on the Appleson project. It is important for us to establish an absolute top figure that we will not exceed."
>
> "Paulette, I thought we agreed that this project was mine to run as I saw fit. If you're gonna ride herd on me, you might as well take it over yourself."
>
> "You know, John, we've both got some concerns about this. You're letting me know that it feels like I'm interfering. I'm trying to let you know how worried I am about the budget that I'm accountable for. What do you say that we set aside about an hour when we can do this thing some justice?"

"Okay, when?"

"How about this afternoon from 3 to 4 o'clock in your office?"

"Uh, let's see, I was going to give Maggie some dictation then, but it can wait. Alright, let's make it at 3 o'clock. Maybe we can both clear the air."

The informal agenda can also be combined with your response time records (see chapter 3). Consider the following example:

"Dr. Edmond, I'm calling to see if we can change the time of our meeting tomorrow from 2 o'clock to 6 o'clock."

"Six o'clock, Mrs. Weston? I'm afraid that wouldn't work for the members of our staff. Is there a problem with 2 o'clock?"

"Actually, there is. You see, our attorney can only be present at 6 o'clock."

"Mrs. Weston, I need to reclarify with you the purpose of this meeting as far as we are concerned. We will be happy to advise you of why our firm has dropped your merchandise from our line. We are doing this as a favor to you since you indicated you wanted to learn from what you admitted to be your company's mistakes. We are not interested in participating in this meeting if you have any other purposes in mind."

"Well, Dr. Edmond, I was informed by Mrs. Jenkins, who you spoke with yesterday, that you intended to negotiate new terms with us during the meeting."

"Mrs. Weston, I have my record of that conversation directly in front of me. I specifically stated to Mrs. Jenkins that we would be happy to meet with you personally to help you understand what your salesman did that led us to our decision to end our business relationship with you. The purpose for the meeting as far as we are concerned is to give you this information. If that purpose is not acceptable to you, if you have any other purposes in mind, or if you intend to have anyone else present besides you and Mrs. Jenkins, we will not meet with you. Given that set of conditions, would you still like to meet tomorrow?"

Procedural Guidelines for the Informal Agenda

1. Establish a purpose for the meeting that all participants will agree upon.
2. Determine the date, location, and beginning-ending times for the meeting.
3. Record the details regarding the purpose and the scheduling items in your response time binder (see Chapter 3). Schedule the meet-

ing as needed in your job-list binder and daily calendar (see Chapter 7).

4. Summarize the discussion and the decisions reached during the meeting to verify that each of the participants are in agreement as to the content of what was expressed.

5. Record the summary in your response time binder. Include details as to who was present, what issues were discussed, which specific decisions were reached, what action will be taken—by when, by whom, and any followup measures to check on progress. Schedule any workload that results from the meeting in your job-list binder and daily calendar.

The rules pertaining to setting the agenda provide guidelines for how to prepare people for a meeting. The meeting might be informal or formal and it might involve two people or large numbers of participants that comprise a complex work team. A carefully planned agenda will help to access the ego of each participant so as to foster participation and cooperation and to minimize behaviors that are defensive, aggressive, and self-serving. Setting the agenda, therefore, is designed to help the leader get each of the participants in a cooperative and productive frame of mind before the meeting actually begins.

SPEAKING BEFORE A GROUP

Your success in projecting an image of leadership and in becoming recognized as a representative of your organization will depend in large part on your competence in speaking. You will need to strike a delicate balance between sounding like an authority on the one hand and sounding overbearing and self-centered on the other. There are four basic steps to follow when you want a group of people to recognize you as an authority on the podium. First, get their attention. Second, spell out your objectives. Third, tell them what you expect them to do in order to accomplish your objectives. Finally, let them know what success or failure at accomplishing your objectives will mean to them.

Most authorities who council executives in the area of effective speaking agree on the following guidelines:

Strive to develop trust and rapport. The better able you are to put people at ease, the easier it is to communicate with them. Give the impression that your listeners are the focus of your attention. By engaging each one personally, you will be effectively decreasing their own tensions and thereby reduce the emotional distance between you and them (Sager, 1974).

Become an informed speaker. By increasing your depth of knowledge (information from your field) and your breadth of knowledge (information outside your field), you will become more informed. Keep up on current events by reading daily newspapers and weekly and monthly magazines, listening to news broadcasts, and by seeking information through questioning well-informed acquaintances. The more interests that you share with other people, the more comfortable they will feel with you (Hunsaker & Alessandra, 1980).

Establish control of your listeners by capturing their attention. Create a clash between what people expect to happen and the actual event itself. For example, symbols of violence in a peaceful environment or calm attitudes in an atmosphere of chaos attract attention because of the stark contrasts. Similarly, you should create some sort of conflict initially for your listeners that you will eventually resolve for them. The emotional force will then hold their attention. Make sure that it is held together through a strong theme that has a solid purpose. Dramatize, humanize, and illustrate colorfully to convey that you are a real person who is truly in touch with the down to earth needs of the organization (Boettinger, 1979).

Use specific details to substantiate your major points. Fill your discussion with picturesque speech that converts your personal experiences into conversational expressions. Illustrate your competence with clear and concise language, coherence of thought, and high energy levels to explain your specialized areas of knowledge and to deliver professional sets of instruction (Carnegie, 1977).

Organize your thinking as a way to organize your delivery. Prepare your presentation well in advance even if your interaction will be considered informal. Remember, you will be under constant scrutiny. Drill yourself on what comments you can work into specific topics and bombard yourself with questions that have even the smallest chance of being asked. Fit your subject to the time, arrange your thoughts into a logical sequence, back up your points with facts and figures and then turn these facts into pictures that will enhance the prospect's ability to understand and remember them. Work intensively so that you can think analytically on the spur of the moment. Then fit anticipated questions into the categories around which you prepare yourself to address. Speak to the points immediately, vigorously, and confidently. Use examples to capture attention including brief stories that have a beginning, middle, and end. Keep your comments tied to your central theme, do not stray, and limit yourself to as few words as possible (Sarnoff, 1982).

Polish your speech. Listen to yourself over a tape recorder and realize that the playback is really the way you sound to everyone except yourself. Speak at your lowest comfortable pitch, but do not strain. Support your voice with plenty of breath. Rid your speech of unnecessary words and nervous expressions. Catch and eliminate the "you know," "uh," "kind of," "sort of," and "don't you think" hedges that detract from your image of authority. Your speech must direct and inform with energy, clarity, and momentum. In addition, quiet yourself down by eliminating nervous habits such as cracking your knuckles, bouncing your crossed leg over the other, tapping your fingers, or twitching a moustache, beard, or strands of hair. Start observing yourself for these habits. If you are nervous, deal with it constructively. In general, be on time, use the correct pronunciation of everyone's name, walk into the room with a sense of vitality, listen thoughtfully, look at the people with whom you are conversing, ask relevant, but noninflammatory questions, and most importantly, be pleasant to be around (Sarnoff, 1981).

GIVING DIRECTIONS

The members of the work team require clear and specific directions from the person in charge. The directions should focus on the task that needs to be accomplished. The directions should be preceded with a statement of purpose so that the subordinate understands the reasons as to why and how his or her work will be part of a team effort and how the team's efforts will contribute to the welfare of the company. The directions themselves should be presented in a series of brief statements. The statements should be given in the order in which they are to be performed. The leader should summarize the directions after the specific details have been presented. The subordinates should then be asked to summarize their understanding of the directions. This summary will allow the leader to correct any misunderstandings and will enable him or her to address any questions from the subordinates.

The leader should present the directions through the use of brief, direct, and action-oriented sentences. These statements should indicate what the subordinate is to do, in what order, and by when. The leader should not only convey that he or she is decisive, but equally important, that he or she regards the members of the work team with dignity and respect. Examples of such statements are:

> "I want you to call Murdock. Tell him that we have decided to challenge their pricing structure. Give him a chance to react and have his say. Listen to him. Confirm that you understood his position by summarizing the main points that he made to you. Let him know that we are willing to negotiate. Arrange a meeting with them in our offices sometime next week."

> "I have decided to send you to the training program. You are to report to the session on Monday morning at 8:00 A.M. Let me know

your opinion on how the concepts compare with our analysis that we reviewed during the meeting last week."

"I am taking you off of the Jekert project. I need you to work with the galvinizing engineers before they draft their plans for the Masterson highrise. I want you to report to them by the beginning of next week. Oh, I would like you to detail the progress you've made so far with the Jekert people. Take your time with it, though. Just make sure I see it before the end of the quarter."

In each example, the directions are clear, direct, and decisive. The statements are brief and are sequenced in the order that the work is to be performed. The subordinate should have no difficulty in following the directions since their specificity leaves little room for misinterpretation. Note that the directions indicate exactly what the leader expects the subordinate to do. They do not ask for the subordinate's approval nor do they convey that the leader is apologetic, indecisive, insecure, or overly permissive. Furthermore, the statements do not express impulsiveness, aggression, or rigidity. Instead, they are assertive in that they express what the leader intends for the subordinate to do in a manner that does not attack the subordinate's self-worth. Following the presentation of the directions, the leader can deal with the subordinate's reactions through open-ended questions, summaries, reflective listening, and other forms of superego desensitizers.

Procedural Guidelines for Giving Directions

1. Precede the directions with a statement of purpose.
2. Focus the directions specifically on the tasks that need to be accomplished.
3. Present the directions in a series of brief statements.
4. Sequence the directions in the order that they are to be performed.
5. Summarize the directions after the specific details have been presented.
6. Have the subordinate summarize his or her understanding of what he or she is expected to do and in what order.
7. Correct any misunderstandings and address questions; reconfirm that there is mutual understanding of any modifications from the original set of directions.

ANNOUNCING POLICIES

Policies may be developed through any number of channels. The members of the work team may participate in the formulation of policies, the policies may be determined autocratically by the leader, or they may be developed by work teams that represent the leader's own superiors. Regardless of their origin, the leader's responsibility is to inform the work team of the creation, revision, and termination of policies that either directly or indirectly affect the work team. The subordinates often feel a greater sense of involvement if the leader helps them understand the reasons as to why policies have changed. The procedures for participative policy development will be discussed shortly (see Decision Making). For now, the important point is to remember that a vital function of leadership is to keep members of the work team fully informed of policy status.

Procedural Guidelines for Announcing Policies

1. Announce policy developments and changes with direct and simple statements.
2. Discuss the rationale for why the changes were considered to be a necessity.
3. Indicate the key personnel who were involved in determining the policy changes by using factual, noninflammatory statements.
4. Give the members of the work team an opportunity to discuss the changes especially if the implementation of the changes is beyond their control.
5. Allow adequate time for the members of the work team to adapt to the changes by announcing them well in advance of their implementation.

MANAGING INTERRUPTIONS

You must retain your control of the power to lead at all times. If your subordinates are allowed to take power away from you, your ability to maintain your authority will have been compromised. Interruptions represent one means by which you could very easily lose your control.

The most effective way to deal with an interruption is to identify it at the very instant it occurs. To allow an interruption to continue, whether intentionally or by default, risks the prospect of a snowball effect in which the original interruption could spawn chain reactions from other members, all attempting to have their own say in their own defense. The procedure then is to first acknowledge the person who interrupts the discussion. Call the person by name, cordially but firmly. Indicate that you will have to stop the person from proceeding. Express your understanding that he or she has some strong concerns that he or she wants to make known. Assure the person that there will be an opportunity to do so before the consideration of the current issue is closed.

Your intervention must be swift, brief, and expressed with a decisive tone of voice. At the same time, your voice should carry a ring of warmth in conveying your understanding of how important the subordinate's opinion is to him or her personally. Think of yourself as similar to the conductor of an orchestra. You must be in control of the timing during interactions. You alone will signal who is to talk, what the topic will be, and for what duration. Yet you must also balance your directiveness with compassion for the variety of feelings that will undoubtedly be stirring within the members of your work team. Your skills must keep their ego accessed as much as possible. As the frustrations of work team members reach their limits, you must be able to desensitize team members sufficiently so as to bring their egos back on line. The following example will illustrate these concepts:

LEADER (JOAN):	After the salesman places the customer's order, I want production to fill it within ten days, not the traditional four weeks that . . .
SUBORDINATE (RICK):	Wait a minute! Sales has delayed turning in the orders so they can boost their commissions at the end of the month. I don't know about the rest of you, but I don't think its fair that we . . .
LEADER:	Rick, I need to stop you. You have some strong objections to changing our scheduling, right?
RICK:	Absolutely!
LEADER:	And there are quite a few things you want me to know about how Sales has been running their operation?
RICK:	That's putting it mildly.
LEADER:	Fair enough. I agree that these concerns should be addressed. Right now, I need to put them on hold. I'll get back to them in a few minutes. Let's refocus for the moment on whether or not the prospect of rescheduling is within the physical limits of the machinery. Considering the results from our last calibration, I wonder if . . .

The example illustrates that the leader reacted to the interruption immediately, firmly, and with decisiveness. At the same time, she used superego desensitizers to reassure the subordinate's id that there was no danger. The acknowledgement of the subordinate's concerns provided temporary relief from the anxiety that had been building up. The relief brought about a reduction in the anxiety levels and enabled energy to flow to the subordinate's ego. With his ego accessed, the subordinate could then tolerate the wait for his turn. In the meantime, he could hear the information that the leader wanted him and the other members of the work team to consider.

Procedural Guidelines for Managing Interruptions

1. Be prepared to stop the interruption as soon as it occurs.
2. Acknowledge the person who interrupts by name.
3. Indicate that you will have to stop the person from proceeding.
4. Express your understanding that he or she has some strong concerns that he or she wants to make known.
5. Assure the person that there will be an opportunity to do so before the consideration of the current topic is closed.
6. Refocus the discussion back to the topic at hand.

DECISION MAKING

When the normal and expected functions of the working relationship break down, the leader must intervene to restore stability. The relationship life cycle predicts that periods of instability will occur in all relationships. The instability is triggered by a jolt. The jolt is a conflict that arises when one person within the relationship acts in a manner that is inconsistent with the other person's expectations. Recall that the subordinates formed the expectations during the early phases of the relationship's development. Only a relatively small portion of each individual's personal characteristics were actually exposed during the early developmental phases. The commitment that the individuals made to one another rested on an important assumption. The assumption was that they had come to know one another—that there would be no surprises about the other person that might pop out one day and cause unexpected frustration or grief.

In reality, of course, people are not static. One person can never fully know another at any given time. Nor can any person remain constant and entirely predictable in his or her desires and behaviors over a period of time. Therefore, the normal functions that occur within a working relationship will, at some point, break down whenever the members fail to live up to one another's expectations. The typical reaction is to blame the dysfunction on the other person. Few people understand the dynamics of how relationships can be expected to follow this predictable course and as such, are totally unprepared to deal with the outcome.

The leader's function is to restore the stability so that normal work functions can either resume or be modified in accordance with negotiations over changing roles. The objective is to move the relationship from the period of instability back to a period of stability as quickly and effectively as possible. Two ways by which the leader can attempt to restore stability are through arbitration and team decision making; each a unique form of decision making.

Arbitration

Arbitration is a form of problem solving in which the leader arrives at unilateral decisions after weighing evidence from all parties involved. The leader prepares an agenda, listens to representatives from each side, decisively manages interruptions, provides feedback to verify understanding of the issues, and then announces a decision in the same manner that he would announce policies. As an executive, the leader's power will support his capacity to arrive at the decisions, to implement them, and to make certain that all members of the work team abide by them (see Figure 5–1).

There are two potential complications that the leader should consider when using arbitration as a method for decision making. The first problem is that the leader's decision may in effect be a superego trigger for the members of the nonsupported side. The leader could attempt to minimize this outcome by using the procedures designed for giving

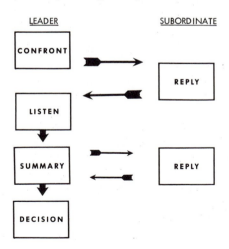

FIG. 5-1 A Leader's Guide To Arbitrative Decision Making

criticism (see chapter 4). In other words, support the nonsupported side through the careful use of superego desensitizers. In addition, the leader can follow up her decisions by meetings with the nonsupported members that give them an opportunity to ventilate their reactions. Nonetheless, the use of arbitration risks aggressive or passive-aggressive responses from the nonsupported members—both towards the leader and towards the members of the supported side.

The second potential complication is that while the leader gets input about the problem from both sides, the ideas for resolving the problem generally stem from adversarial rather than from cooperative principles. In other words, instead of stimulating both sides to think creatively towards solutions that could be of mutual benefit, the arbitrator may inadvertently stimulate each side to advance its own position by attacking the position of its counterpart. The outcome may be a decision that causes more complications than workable alternatives. Solutions that could have satisfied both parties might remain dormant, unexpressed, or completely overlooked.

Team Decision Making

Team decision making is a process that incorporates the participation of everyone involved in the dispute. Solutions stem from interaction among the team members rather than from an arbitrator's unilateral decisions (see Figure 5–2). The method involves the strategic (pre-planned) use of six specific steps. The appropriate implementation of the steps enables the leader to access the ego of all of the parties so that

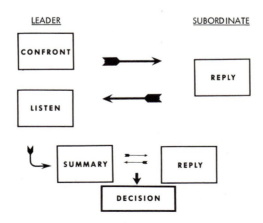

FIG. 5-2 A Leader's Guide To Team Decision Making

order can be preserved and solutions can be developed from the prudent thinking of everyone concerned.

The six steps of the team decision-making process are (Gordon, 1978):

1. Defining the problem
2. Proposing solutions
3. Analyzing the proposals
4. Choosing a solution
5. Determining an action plan
6. Assessing the results

Prior to discussing the problem itself, each of the participants should have received a written agenda or at least have considered the details of the meeting with the leader herself. The leader should call the meeting to order precisely at the prearranged starting time. Depending upon the degree of formality, the leader can use statements such as "We have a quorum and the first item of business is . . ." or simply "It's time to begin." The essential purpose of the opening statement is to rechannel attention from the premeeting conversations into the business at hand. The leader must make this transition decisively so that the attention of each participant falls under her control.

If there are rules that the leader expects the participant to observe, this is the time to specify them. It is often useful to delineate the rules for direct participation in the meeting. For example, the leader may indicate that she will allow ample time for each member to present his or her own views and time for questions, comments, and disagreement. However, the leader will specify when each of these times will occur:

> "I realize this is a sensitive issue that impacts each of us in this room. We all have strong feelings that we no doubt want to express. I need to let you know now, though, that I can only listen to one person at a time. I will not allow interruptions to get us off the topic, nor will I permit side conversations to distract us from what we are trying to accomplish. I expect us to work together and I will do everything that I can to make sure that no one's individual needs dominate the welfare of everyone else."

Defining the Problem.   Once the leader has established his position as the director of the meeting, and that order will flow from his control, it is time to begin *defining the problem*. Effective resolution of any problem depends largely upon understanding the specific issues that have been creating difficulties. The leader's first step is to invite or select someone to present the issue from his or her own perspective: "Tell me about the problem as you see it." All the rules that have applied to listening also apply here. The leader should prevent interruptions from occurring, acknowledge the speaker's various points with nonverbal support, use door opening questions, and reflect content and feelings.

The essential objective is to develop an understanding of the issue from the participant's perspective. The objective is not to change that perspective. The necessity for change may actually represent one possible solution to the problem. However, this is not the time to discuss solutions. This phase of the process is specifically for identifying the aspects of the problem, not yet to solve the problem. Solutions, at this point, would be premature, volatile, and highly unstable. If someone begins to suggest or perhaps argue over what should be done, intervene immediately, reflect their concern, indicate that the concern will be addressed shortly, and then refocus the discussion on what had preceded the interruption.

Once the subordinate has presented her major concerns, summarize them, ask if she would like to add any other points, and then proceed to the next participant. By following this course, you will establish the details that comprise the problem in all the various dimensions and perspectives. In addition, you will have prevented emotions from causing further complications by reframing interruptions as expressions of frustration and concern and by refocusing the issues from those emotions back to the principal business at hand.

The final step in this first phase of team problem solving is to summarize the discussion from each of the participants. Once again, ask if anyone would like to add to his or her presentations. Do not proceed until all persons agree that you have understood their various positions and that they have mentioned everything that needs to be considered. With all of the concerns expressed and documented, you are ready to begin discussing possible solutions.

Proposing Solutions. Throughout the team decision-making process, the leader must continually apply her knowledge of human temperament. Part of the reason that this process is divided into steps is to help the participants determine workable solutions in a structured rather than a chaotic and disorganized manner. This structure contributes to ego operations among participants. The process also contributes to organized thinking in that it separates creative thinking from analytic thinking.

Think about this concept for a minute. How do you feel when you come up with an idea that someone else ridicules? Even if you could admit that your idea probably would not have worked, you tend to become defensive. More than likely, your reaction to this person would be a negative one. At best, you would probably clam up and stop trying to make any further contributions. In other words, the person's critical reaction to your idea was actually a superego trigger that flooded your ego with anxiety. Overcome by this anxiety, your ego lost its capacities for creative thinking and gave way to the impulsive behaviors of the id.

By separating the process of brainstorming from analysis, the leader effectively orchestrates the modes of thinking among the subordinates. The separation facilitates ego operations which in effect support prudent instead of irrational and self-defensive thinking.

The leader indicates that he wants everyone to think of any solution that might have even a remote chance of solving the problems. It is important to encourage people to suggest any and all possibilities. Reassure them not to worry about how the suggestions might sound or what other people might think about them. Inform them that the most effective solutions are often born from the bits and pieces of what otherwise might have been tossed aside as irrelevant or unimportant.

An often useful approach to the brainstorming process is the "timed" approach. Instruct everyone to get ready to write down as many possible solutions that they can think of as soon as you give them the signal. Tell them you will call "time" at the end of one minute (or whatever brief period you may choose). You might assign the same task to the entire group or assign subgroups to work on different aspects of the problem. If you work within subgroups, perhaps you might have the individual members in each subgroup come up with their own ideas first, and then expand them by comparison and discussion in the subgroup. Finally, spokespersons from the subgroups can report their ideas to the group at large.

The use of dividing a large group into smaller task-focused groups can be extremely effective in accomplishing desired results. Performance by an individual within a small group is often much less stressful than in front of larger numbers of people. In many cases, the number and quality of proposed solutions will be significantly enhanced by the formation of small groups.

The central concept that underlies the success of group participation pertains to the maintenance of order. Give the groups instructions *one step at a time*. Imagine what would happen if you gave one long series of instructions to a large group that they would have to retain for their work in their small groups. You will lose them. Tell them the first thing you want them to do. Then, allow them time to do it. Next, give them the second instruction followed immediately by time to accomplish the results. Throughout the process, order will be preserved and you will remain in charge.

In some cases, participants will have difficulty thinking of or contributing any possible solutions that they would like to propose. You can often facilitate the creative process by using door openers. Use statements that encourage their consideration of the problems that have been identified:

> I wonder what might make some sense from your point of view.
> I really would like to know what you've considered.
> I'm curious as to what people have thought of that they have already decided just won't work.

When you begin eliciting the proposals from the participants, make sure that you prevent interruptions. Remind them that the purpose in this phase of the process is to develop as many ideas as possible. Whether or not the proposals can be considered feasible is a separate matter that will be up for discussion in the next phase. If you do not separate the process of creative thinking from that of analysis, negative reactions to proposals will elicit the superego trigger in the contributor and subseqently cut off the creative process. Other participants will feel stifled for fear of being ridiculed. Maintain a high level of energy among the participants to facilitate a high output of contribution. Quantity is what counts at this stage. Quality will be carved out from the proposals during the next stage.

Analyzing the Proposal. After the groups have finished their assigned tasks, call them back together and make a central list of all of the proposed solutions that the groups have suggested. After the list has been compiled, you can begin evaluating each of the proposals. Keep the discussion operating from the focus of the ego. Prevent interruptions from breaking down the working process. Focus comments on the extent to which each proposal can solve all aspects of the problem from all perspectives. You are working towards assessing the proposals in terms of how well they address the specific problems that have been identified. The objective is to arrive at a *consensus* as to which proposals will meet everyone's needs versus those that will not.

You may need to conduct negotiations at this point as to how specific items regarding any given proposal might need to be changed in order for it to best serve everyone involved. During the process of negotiation, prevent interruptions, use door openers, and summarize positions. Then, resolve differences by facilitating compromise and accommodation to the extent that the opposing participants agree would make matters workable.

Choosing a Solution. During this phase, you will help the participants select one, two, or any combination of the listed proposals that will resolve the work-related difficulties. The selection often comes down to a type of "best fit" agreement. It is important to stress the flexibility of this process. In other words, convey the attitude that the agreement you may reach will not be cast in concrete. Instead, the work team will implement it for a period of time to see how it works. If it does not resolve the problem or perhaps even creates complications, further negotiations can always be arranged. Consider using statements such as "I wonder if we can agree to try this possibility out for awhile? Can each one of you live with it until we can see how it works out?" Usually, this call for flexibility facilitates cooperation from even the most resistant group members.

Determining an Action Plan. Once the participants have decided upon the proposals they intend to adopt, it is important to develop an action plan. The action plan needs to specify all the steps necessary for the solution to be implemented. The items for discussion might include determining who will be involved, when steps will need to occur, what will have to be ordered or repaired, how much money will have to be spent, what complications might arise, and so forth. Before the meeting ends, each participant should be absolutely certain as to what his or her responsibilities are for implementing the plan.

The final step in the planning process is to schedule a meeting to assess how the solution will have worked out. Taking the time to schedule the meeting assures everyone that the solution can later be modified in the event that it does not live up to everyone's expectations.

Assessing the Results. The purpose of this meeting is, of course, to determine the effectiveness of the solutions that were proposed and implemented earlier. Each participant or spokesperson presents the issues individually that are then integrated and summarized by the leader. The benefits and the costs of the solutions are considered by the group at large or by subgroups as needed. Modifications can be negotiated if necessary. The ultimate objective is to arrive at a consensus as to the viability of the solution. Additional assessment meetings can be scheduled if warranted by the results from the discussion. By the end of the process thus far, the work team will have either solved its problem, agreed to further negotiations on a specific solution, or agreed to conduct the process from a fresh start.

The main objective in team decision making is to enable a work team to solve its own problems through structured participation. The leader's role is to actively maintain order throughout the process so that *reasonable actions* can be given a fair chance to determine the outcomes of working relationships.

Procedural Guidelines for
Team Decision Making

1. Ask someone to begin the discussion by defining the problem from his or her own perspective.
2. Prevent interruptions from occurring, acknowledge each of the speaker's points, use door-opening inquiries, and reflect content and emotion.
3. Encourage participants to suggest any and all possibilities for solving the problem.
4. Assess the proposals in terms of how well they address the specific problems that have been identified.
5. Help the participants select one, two, or any combination of proposals that have the best chance of resolving the difficulties.
6. Develop an action plan that specifies how the proposals will become reality.
7. Conduct a follow-up meeting to evaluate the results. Recycle the team problem-solving process as necessary.

CONSEQUENCES FOR UNSATISFACTORY PERFORMANCE

In attempting to maintain the stability of working relationships, the leader will encounter dysfunctions that interfere with effective work performance. Earlier discussions have referred to these dysfunctions as "jolts." The leader can attempt to restore stability by persisting in efforts to resolve the jolts with the specific people involved. Using the Relationship Life Cycle as a model, the leader can apply the principles of team decision making to reclarify roles and to redefine expectations with the subordinate in question. In other words, the subordinate will be given an opportunity to account for unsatisfactory performance, negotiate methods by which to satisfy his or her needs, and ultimately restore efficiency to his or her work performance.

During the assessment meeting that will follow the problem-solving process, the leader will review the status of the subordinate's current work performance. If the performance has not improved to the leader's satisfaction, the subordinate must be advised of the consequences he will face for continued nonconformance to the leader's expectations. Recall that a business cannot succeed if its workers drain instead of contribute to its resources. As such, advising the subordinate of the consequences for unsatisfactory performance paints a picture of the reality that both the leader and the subordinate must face. Following this confrontation, the leader will invite the subordinate to participate once again in the process of team decision making. In other words, the leader will have actually given the subordinate two separate opportunities to make his own wants and needs known and to negotiate for their consideration. If the subordinate's performance has not satisfied the leader's expectations following the second opportunity for team decision making, the leader must then administer the consequences without further consideration or prolonged delay.

Procedural Guidelines
Administering Consequences
for Unsatisfactory Performance

1. Manage dysfunctions in working relationships by first defining the problem in a discussion with the subordinate. Negotiate agreements regarding your expectations and the subordinate's roles and responsibilities within the working relationship.
2. If the subordinate does not abide by the agreement that stemmed from the negotiations, advise him of the consequences he will face if dysfunctional performance continues.
3. Offer the subordinate an additional opportunity to resolve the problem through further discussion and negotiations with you.
4. Administer the consequences if the subordinate's subsequent work performance remains at substandard levels.

SUMMARY

The procedures in this chapter have been classified as advanced communication skills. In fulfilling the responsibilities in the areas of representing the organization, the leader will need to develop platform skills. To successfully take charge of a group of people, the leader will need to set an agenda, give directions, announce policies, and manage interruptions. The process of making decisions that will determine the organization's stability and growth will be enhanced when the leader seeks input from concerned people. The procedures for arbitrative and team decision making will facilitate this process. Finally, the leader must confront individual's whose performance could potentially drain the organization of its resources. Though never a pleasant task, the procedures for administering consequences will provide a helpful structure for meeting this responsibility.

TOPICS FOR DISCUSSION

1. Describe the differences between a formal and an informal agenda and discuss the situations that are appropriate for each type.
2. Many executives have reported that their greatest fear is speaking before a group of people. What measures would you suggest to help them overcome this fear?
3. Imagine that you were leading a group discussion on the subject of next year's budget. Two members of your group are mumbling something about how you mismanaged funds in the past. How would you handle this interruption?
4. What are the differences between arbitrative and team decision making? When is it appropriate to use one versus the other?
5. Describe a leader you know who would have a difficult time confronting a subordinate whose performance was unsatisfactory. What measures could you suggest to help this leader deal effectively and fairly with the subordinate?

RECOMMENDED READINGS

BOETTINGER, H. M. (1979). *Moving mountains or the art of letting others see things your way.* New York: Collier Macmillan.

CALLANAN, J. (1984). *Communicating: How to organize meetings and presentations.* New York: Watts.

DAVIS, J. (1954). *Handbook of sales training.* Englewood Cliffs, NJ: Prentice-Hall.

GORDON, T. (1978). *Leader effectiveness training.* Solana Beach, CA: Effectiveness Training Inc.

HUGENBERG, L., & YODER, D. (1985). *Speaking skills in the modern organization.* Glenview, IL: Scott, Foresman and Company.

MCCORMACK, M. (1984). *What they don't teach you at Harvard Business School.* New York: Bantam.

NIERENBERG, G. (1973). *Fundamentals of negotiating.* New York: Hawthorn Books, Inc.

SARNOFF, D. (1981). *Make the most of your best.* New York: Doubleday.

CHAPTER SIX
CASE STUDIES: PROBLEMS AND SOLUTIONS

OUTLINE

INTRODUCTION
THE CASE OF TOM DEMERIST

    The Problem
    The Solution

THE CASE OF BEVERLY JACOBY

    The Problem
    The Solution

THE CASE OF JERRY WILLIAMS

    The Problem
    The Solution

SUMMARY
TOPICS FOR DISCUSSION

INTRODUCTION

In this chapter we will learn how to apply the skills that have been presented from the earlier chapters. Before we approach the cases in terms of problems and solutions, let's become better acquainted with the cast of characters.

In the first case, Tom Demerist and his wife Susan just moved into a very exclusive home in a very exclusive subdivision. They were fortunate to have developed a retail business that enabled them to make the house payments. Soon after they moved in, Tom attended a subdivision meeting where he learned about some rather serious problems that were jeopardizing the stability of the entire subdivision. The current president of the board of trustees resigned leaving the board without leadership or direction. By the time the meeting ended, Tom found himself elected as the new president. The entire subdivision, not to mention his own family, now depended upon him to take charge of an extremely difficult situation.

The second case involves an administrative nurse, Beverly Jacoby. Beverly directed the division of Nursing Services in a home health agency. The nursing staff that reported to Beverly was responsible for providing home care to patients who had just been discharged from the hospital. Generally, the nurses encountered a great deal of hostility among the patients and their families when they arrived in their homes to offer their nursing services. The problem in this case revolves around a series of misrepresentations that the nurses attributed to unethical practices within the division of Patient Relations. Similar to a marketing force, the personnel from Patient Relations signed patients up for the group's services. Supposedly, they promised that the patients would receive treatment from nursing specialists such as cardiac care nurses and neurological nurses. The patients became very upset when licensed practical nurses arrived. These nurses took the brunt of the hostility directly from the patients. In turn they unleashed their anger on their director, Beverly Jacoby. Beverly has tried unsuccessfully to solve the problem. As the case begins, many of the nurses are refusing to follow Beverly's policies. Beverly's ultimatum is that either they comply or they will be fired.

The final case revolves around a conflict between a newly promoted manager and an executive officer who opposed the promotion. Jerry Williams was an accountant with a prestigious accounting firm. He made the company a great deal of money from his expertise in accounting. As a reward, two of the three partners promoted him to management. The third partner, John Kensington, fought the promotion every step of the way. The case portrays the difficulties that occur when an individual achieves recognition and power as an authority without having the competence to back it up. The story reaches its climax when Kensington directly confronts Jerry after a minority worker claimed Jerry discriminated against her.

Each case will be presented in two parts. First, the problem will be portrayed. As the events unfold, retrace your steps through the principles and procedures from the previous chapters. Try to remember the phases from the relationship life cycle. Ask yourself how the characters established their roles and their expectations of one another. When did jolts first occur? What were the superego triggers that caused them to develop? How did the members of the relationship handle the conflicts? Were the leaders able to access their own egos or did they fall victim to superego-id battles? What might they have done differently at the point when instability first interfered with the productivity in the working relationship. What basic and advanced communication skills could they have applied to redirect the tension and anxieties from impulsive behaviors into productive channels?

The second part of the case will portray how the leaders solved the problems in each case. Initially, the leader will access his or her own ego and then attempt to desensitize the superegos of the work team members. Once the egos are accessed, the leader will give directions, set policies, or make decisions using the skills presented from the earlier chapters. Try to anticipate what skills the leader in each case will attempt to apply before you actually read what they did. Refer back to the chapters to get help.

The Case of Tom Demerist

The Problem

Tom and Susan Demerist pulled into their driveway just as it was getting dark. Susan pressed the garage door opener while Tom inched the car slowly toward the house. Just as he was about to drive the car into the garage, Tom noticed a piece of paper fluttering down from the rising door.

"I'll get it," Susan said, as she opened her door and got out to retrieve the paper. She glanced at it in front of the car, but realized that there wasn't enough sunlight to make out any of the print.

Tom and Susan had just moved into their new house in the Lakeside View Estates. For both, this home had been years in the planning. They had worked jointly with the architect and a builder for months before the construction team even broke ground. It was truly a dream house for both of them. Michelle, now 7, and Adam, who had just turned 4, were both too young to appreciate the sacrifices their parents had made to get them into a school system that would virtually secure their admission to an Ivy League college. Building the house nearly exhausted Tom and Susan's short-term investment accounts and left just a few thousand in liquid savings in case of an emergency. Several years ago they quit their jobs and bought a franchise of a nationally known book store. It was a big step with risks that almost scared them out of making the decision. Tom gave up his position at a university and Susan left her managerial position in a local department store. The risks paid off. They made a great deal of money over a period of seven years. They invested all of it in funds that they would use to build their dream home. The business continued to grow, and now, at last, they lived in Lakeside View Estates.

"What does it say?" Tom asked.

"Something about a neighborhood meeting," Susan replied. "I can't make all of it out. I think the rain must have smeared it. 'URGENT—Tonight at 7:30 in the clubhouse. If you can't attend, contact . . . ' . The rest of it is washed out. Tom, we can't go. Michelle's teacher set up a special appointment for us at 7:30 so she could go over the curriculum and show us around the school. We can't cancel that. She stayed after hours just to accommodate us."

Tom parked the car, took the keys out of the ignition, and sat back. "Susan, this neighborhood meeting must be important. One of us should be there. Would you be upset if you went to see Mrs. Selby by yourself? I really want to find out what's going on around here and why this meeting is so urgent."

"It's all right," Susan said reassuringly. She sat quietly for a moment. "I really am disappointed though. Having Michelle in this school was something we both wanted."

"I know," Tom said. "Please tell Mrs. Selby what happened and that I am looking forward to meeting her."

Tom was uneasy during dinner. The kids horsed around at the table which unnerved Tom and Susan to no end. But it was more than that that bothered Tom. He couldn't put the meeting out of his mind. For some reason, it threatened him.

He helped Susan clear the table and finish the dishes. He gave her a hug, put on his coat, reread the note and once more tried to make out the print on the message that had been washed out. Still, he had no luck with it. He said good night to Michelle and Adam and then told Susan he figured he would see her around ten.

Tom got to the clubhouse at about 7:25. He was greeted by one of his next-door neighbors, Terry Waterman. "Any idea what's going on, Tom?" Terry asked.

"I was about to ask you the same thing," Tom replied. "Susan and I tried to call you and Jeanne, but I guess you just got home a few minutes before the meeting."

Several other people came into the clubhouse at the same time. Jim Henderson, the vice president of the board of trustees asked everyone to sit down so he could call the meeting to order.

"I want to thank all of you for coming on such short notice," Jim said. "I am sorry for being so mysterious in the announcement, but I think you'll soon see what all this is about. There are many things that have recently happened that you need to know about as property owners in Lakeside View Estates. First, Larry Phelps, our board president, called me yesterday to say that he was resigning from the board. He and his family are planning to move out of the subdivision as soon as they can. Their home was vandalized early yesterday morning. The Phelps kept most of their valuables out of the home, but many keepsakes were either taken or defaced. In fact, profanities were plastered on many of the walls and mirrors throughout the house."

Tom raised his hand and was acknowledged by Jim. "I'm Tom Henderson. My wife Susan and I moved in on Lakeside Terrace two days ago. Many of you here have given us a warm welcome and on behalf of my family, I want to say thank you. Jim, I guess I'm somewhat confused. I'm sure its always a scary thing to have your house broken into, and it shakes everyone up to hear about it, but surely that's no reason to move out of a neighborhood."

"Let me go on," Jim said. "As president of the board, Larry received many anonymous complaints from people in the subdivision nearly every day. Residents have been upset about a number of problems in the subdivision for quite a while now.

When they don't get satisfaction, they need to take it out on someone. Larry was the natural target."

"Why Larry?" Tom asked. "Just because he was the head of the board?"

"Well, it was a little more than that," Jim proceeded. "Larry sort of threatened people when they didn't pay their subdivision fees."

"Oh come on, Jim," Al Reily interrupted. "It was more than sort of threatened. He called people 'irresponsible' to their face. He embarrassed husbands in front of their families. He threatened to take them to court. He made a lot of us feel like he was the only decent person around here."

"Wait a minute," Tom said. "This really is beyond me. The homes in this area are in the two hundred thousand dollar bracket. The subdivision fee is $300 a year. What is going on here that people aren't paying it?"

"It's a protest," Sharon Dawson added.

"What do you mean, why a protest?" Tom asked.

"First of all, you have to understand more about this subdivision fee," Jim said. "We need this income to get street lights, to pay for repairs in our pavement, to get the snow removal company out here the same day it snows; and those are just the absolute necessities. We still have to decide what we want to do about building the subdivision pool, to fence in the tennis courts, and to add to the number of trees on the streets. The simple fact is that more than 80 percent of the property owners are in arrears and substantially so at that."

"But why?" Tom pressed.

"Tom, I'm Sharon Dawson. My husband Dave and I were one of the first people to build in Lakeside View Estates. That was five years ago. We were followed by the Wilkinson's, the Reardon's, and the Jackson's."

"You're the folks up in the cul de sac?" Tom asked.

"That's right," Sharon told him. "Anyway, shortly after the cul de sac filled, interest rates and the price of housing began to come down a bit. Within six months, all of the lots on our street sold. Within six months after that, the robberies started to happen. There hasn't been one house that hasn't been robbed on our entire street. I take it back, there is one."

"All right Sharon, hold on," Jim interrupted.

"No, I won't," Sharon insisted. "Tom and his family have every right to know. After all, they live right behind them."

"Behind who?" Tom asked anxiously.

"Sharon, you have no right to stand in judgment," Jim protested. "You have no proof."

"You mean the police won't accept our proof," Sharon insisted. We have eyewitnesses who would swear on Bibles that they saw those kids. And those cars that sit out in front of their house at all hours and then drive out of the subdivision without their lights on when its pitch black. Tom, we're almost sure that the Peterson kids are financing a drug ring by stealing from us in the subdivision."

"Why aren't the police involved?" Tom asked.

"That's just it," Sharon said. "We think they are."

"Sharon, for God sake," Jim said trying to stop her.

"Donald Peterson is the police commissioner," Sharon blurted out. "We have called the police time and again. They come out within minutes, inspect the scene, file their report, and that's the last we hear of it. They tell us that the best thing we can do is to form a Neighborhood Crime Watch that they could supervise. They would help us with the details like inscribing our identification on our valuables and conducting security searches of our homes."

"Sounds like a good idea to me," Tom remarked.

"It is," Jim said. "But Larry was supposed to organize it. I'm afraid that no one trusted him enough anymore to give him the support. He just wasn't cut out to head up our board. The pressure just got to him."

"It's getting to all of us," said Bob Marshall. "Sorry to welcome you to the neighborhood this way, Tom. The fact is that Lakeside View Estates has recently been listed as suffering from the highest crime rate of all the local subdivisions built in the last five years. Aside from the immediate danger to our families and our properties, we all are facing a serious financial loss if this thing causes the value of our homes to go down. We've all got our futures at stake here. Yet we're helpless to do anything about it."

"So we've decided to protest," Sharon's husband Dave told Tom. "We're trying to drive the Peterson's out by taking a stand."

Once again, Jim interrupted. "But don't you see that you all are cutting off your nose to spite your face. We're just hurting one another."

"But if we can hang on together, sooner or later the Peterson's will get the message and leave."

"Oh, come on," Jim said angrily, "hell could freeze over first. In the mean time, we are all suffering without streetlights, or snow removal. Besides that, our streets are all torn up from the construction equipment." Jim paused for a moment. "Look," he said, "it's getting late. We're all tired and frustrated. I called you here to tell you about Larry. As of tomorrow, he's gone. We have no president. We have no leadership. I surely don't want it. We need to elect someone right now."

There was a long silence. Everyone riveted their eyes to the floor dreading that Jim would look at them with expectations. After about two minutes, Sharon raised her hand.

"Sharon, are you volunteering?" Jim asked.

She laughed. "Me, of course not. I could never do it. No, I think we need new blood on this board. I would like to nominate Tom. He's got a stake in this subdivision. He's been asking some intelligent questions all night. Besides that, I happen to know that he and his wife have built one heck of a business up over the last several years. That takes smarts and it takes guts."

The people in the room began to applaud. There was almost a sense of desperation for Tom to accept.

Tom looked over at Sharon for a moment. Then he glanced at his next-door neighbor, Terry. Jim diverted his attention up to the front of the room.

"Tom, what do you say?" Jim asked, almost pleading. "Will you do it?"

"Jim, I don't know what you all expect me to do," Tom replied in frustration.

"That's the irony of it all," Jim said helplessly. "Neither do we. Just take charge somehow and get us out of this mess."

At ten minutes after ten, Tom got home and walked into the kitchen. Susan was having coffee.

"Can I pour you a cup?" she asked warmly.

"That would be nice," Tom said with appreciation.

"Well, what was so urgent that kept you from meeting Mrs. Selby?" she asked innocently.

The Solution

The Relationship Life Cycle.   Tom's relationship began with most of the rest of his neighbors when he met them at the neighborhood meeting. His curiosity and concern about the urgency of the meeting led him to ask a number of questions. This participation indicated to the others there that he wanted to be involved in preserving the welfare of the subdivision. They all, of course, had their financial interests at stake. Tom, however, seemed willing to do something about it. His attitude and manner of speaking, therefore, established his credibility with his neighbors. They needed someone to take over the presidency of their board. Tom fit the bill. There wasn't time to permit their relationship with him to flow through an extended process—that is, becoming acquainted and developing attachments. Some of the neighbors already knew that he had been a college professor, a sign of intelligence and accomplishment in a professional career. Some people also knew of the success he and his wife had in developing and running their own business. Within the course of the meeting, Tom had established his credibility and enabled his new neighbors to become acquainted with him.

The process of defining expectations and clarifying roles with regard to Tom's job as board president would take place during the first meeting he would actually lead. Prior to that, he would have carefully read minutes of previous meetings.

The behavior operating system.   Tom could clearly observe that tension had existed within the subdivision for a considerable period of time. The neighbors' protests over the subdivision fee suggested that the trouble within the subdivision essentially "superego triggered" them. They could no longer think rationally, especially not without an emotionally stable leader to provide a clear sense of direction. Tom's job, then, was to access his own ego, organize the energies from among the neighborhood participants into productive channels, and facilitate a way to solve the problems.

In order for Tom to keep the focus of the group's activities on a reasonable course, he would need to immediately recognize when tensions began to build—that is, superego triggers—and then desensitize the individuals involved in order to access their egos. If Tom ignored the superego triggers, the group's anxieties would be converted by the id component of the personalities involved into impulsively driven behavior. Tom would be able to recognize when this shift occurred as participants would begin to bicker with one another, find scapegoats for their problems, and become easily sidetracked onto very narrowly focused issues. His objective in running his first meeting—and generally in performing his role as board president—is to give the members direction so that they can work together to solve their problems. Unless he actively establishes and maintains control, they will take it away from him. The meeting will then become chaotic, people will leave in anger and frustration, and their problems will likely have become more complicated rather than being resolved.

Tom's work with his neighbors, then, will follow the guidelines for team decision making. He will begin by announcing his agenda. Then he will give a set of directions he expects everyone to follow. He will proceed to enlist the participant's help in identifying the specific problems, next summarize them for the purpose of clarification, and finally move on to eliciting ideas for solutions.

ARRANGEMENTS, PREPARATION, AND INTRODUCTION

Tom scheduled the next subdivision meeting for a week later. He mailed notices to all of the residents in the subdivision; there were 80 of them. Each night during the week before the meeting he made calls to as many of the residents as he could reach between 6:30 and 9:30. He introduced himself, mentioned the names of his family members, and indicated that he had been asked to serve as president of the subdivision's board of trustees. Finally, after briefly getting to know the people he spoke with, he reminded them about the meeting and strongly urged them to attend.

Tom arrived at the clubhouse about 45 minutes before the meeting was scheduled to begin. He arranged the tables in a horseshoe with enough seating for nearly 50 people. He figured that if more came, they could bring extra chairs from the storage room. He made coffee and arranged the cups, spoons, cream, and sugar. "I'm going to have to learn to delegate," he said to himself. "Oh well, at least for this time, I want to make sure everything is set up just the way I want it."

He called the meeting to order exactly at 7:30. He guessed that nearly 40 people were there. The turnout disappointed him somewhat. Nonetheless, these were the people he would work with to get things under control.

He introduced himself and spoke briefly about his family and home. Next, he had everyone pair up with someone from the subdivision that they didn't know. After everyone got situated in their new seats, he instructed the participants to take a couple of minutes to get to know one another. When he called time, he had each person introduce his or her partner to everyone else by name, names of their family members, and where they lived in the subdivision. Tom was pleased. Everyone seemed to enjoy getting to know their "new" neighbors. The activity succeeded in building some cohesiveness.

AGENDA AND DIRECTION

Tom then called for the group's attention. "It's now 7:45," he said. "We will work together tonight until 9:00. First, I want to tell you exactly what I want us to accomplish this evening. Then, I'll let you know what the ground rules are so that we can stay focused on solving the problems that we are all so concerned about.

"I want us to consider tonight as an organizational meeting. We'll start out by bringing everybody up to date on what's been taking place here in this subdivision that has us all so concerned. Let's make sure we agree on all of that first before we try to settle anything. Once I'm sure that we have indentified our problems, then we'll put our heads together to plan how to work on each one of them. We will end the evening by forming working groups that will each have a specific set of tasks to accomplish. Each group will appoint a recorder and spokesperson to present its results to us during our next meeting. By the way, make a note that we will have standing meetings on the first Wednesday night of the month at 7:30 here at the clubhouse until further notice.

"Now, let me tell you about the ground rules for tonight. Everyone who wants to will get a chance to have their say. Considering that feelings are running high about some of the issues we will be discussing, there will be times when you will disagree with what someone else is saying. That's fine. Raise your hand and I'll give you a chance to have your say. If you feel like you need to interrupt somebody, I am going to have to stop you from proceeding until the other person finishes. I hope you won't be offended by that. If you are, I'm sorry. At the same time, I hope you can understand the importance of keeping our discussion focused at all times. Okay, any questions before we begin?" Tom asked. There were none. Tom then continued.

"There were several concerns that were expressed during our meeting last week. They were all new to me since it was my first meeting. Many of you were there. Some of you were not. I'll review them now. Let me know after I have finished if I've overlooked anything." Tom paused to look around the faces in the room. These were the people his family would be getting to know very well over the years. It was important for all of them to believe they could work together.

"Last week Jim Henderson told us that Larry Phelps was resigning as president of our board of trustees. Larry's house had been vandalized. We—or at least I—learned that our subdivision suffered from an extremely high rate of burglaries. Suspicions were that a group of teenagers based within the subdivision were committing the robberies as a way to finance their drug racket. I also came to understand that the local police suggested that the subdivision support a Neighborhood Crime Watch project. The police would help by providing equipment for inscribing owner's names of valuables and by conducting security inspections to help us determine ways to increase our home security. Any comments so far?" Tom asked.

There were none. Tom continued. "Up until now, the Neighborhood Crime Watch has not been organized. As I understand it, everyone was depending on Larry to get people together, but it never happened. Besides the vandalism, we also have concerns about the unrepaired pavements, the delays in snow plowing, the pool that is still on the drawing board, and our tennis courts that need fencing. In order for this work to be done, we need revenue from our subdivision fees. Nearly 80 percent of the property owners in the subdivision have not paid the $300 fee as a protest. The reason for the protest is that the local police commissioner, who happens to live in the subdivision, is also the father of some of the teenage kids who are suspected of the home burglaries. The feeling is that the protest will be an effective way to get our message across to the police commissioner. Have I left anything out?" Tom asked.

Paul Jackson raised his hand and said, "Just for the record, Tom, the revenues from the subdivision fees are also supposed to cover adding to the number of trees in the subdivision."

"Thanks Paul," Tom acknowledged. "Anything else? No, okay, let's go on. What I want to point out is that the protest is one idea we have been using to try to solve our problems. Some of you may think it's a good idea, others may not. Nonetheless, it is one idea. Instead of debating it right now, I want us to start coming up with even more ideas. Once we have made a list of them, we can talk about the ones we can all live with and would be willing to work together on. There will be plenty of time for discussion before we make our decisions. All right, here's what we are going to do. So far, we have been trying to stop the robberies by a protest. The protest has dwindled our subdivision reserves to the point where we cannot pay for some expenses that many of us feel are important. What I want you to consider now is what other ideas to stop the robberies we can come up with that wouldn't restrict our ability to take care of the subdivision's other needs."

INTERRUPTION

Sharon Davis called out, "Tom, you're not giving it time. The protest will work if we wait long enough."

"As you see it, Sharon, the protest can work," Tom reflected. "It's a matter of biting the bullet in a sense. If we can hang in there just a bit longer, the commissioner will get the message."

"Right," Sharon agreed. "He's not a bad person. It's just been real awkward to talk to him. You know, it would sort of be like accusing the man to his face. This way, he'll get the idea. When he does, he'll do something with those kids. The robberies will stop, and then we'll start paying the fee."

REFOCUS TO TASK

"Okay, we've got one idea," Tom said. "Let's get some more. I want you to think of as many other ways to stop the robberies as you can. It's now 8:05. I will give you 5 minutes to write your ideas on the paper in front of you. Abbreviate so you don't waste time writing. This time is for thinking. Don't inhibit yourself by worrying what other people might think. Write down whatever comes to your mind. Ready, begin."

Tom stopped them after exactly 5 minutes. He made a master list on the newsprint board as each person read the ideas. In all, they came up with ten possibilities:

1. Complete the procedures for Neighborhood Crime Watch.
2. Invite the commissioner to a meeting with Tom.
3. Hire a security service to patrol the neighborhood.
4. Invite the boys suspected of the robberies to a meeting with Tom.
5. Report the commissioner to the county supervisor.
6. Establish for sure that the suspected boys are the actual culprits.

7. Phone the license numbers of suspicious cars seen in the subdivision to the local police.
8. Invite the local police to the next subdivision meeting for assistance.
9. Call other subdivision boards to see what they have done when they have had to deal with high crime rates in their area.
10. Continue the protest by not paying subdivision fees.

By 8:30, Tom had completed the master list. He then informed everyone that this was the time to give their opinions on the various ideas. He structured the task by focusing on each idea one at a time. Whenever one person interrupted, he immediately intervened and refocused the discussion on the main topic. By 9 o'clock he was ready to pull everything together.

SUMMARY

"Seems like we've reached a decision," Tom said. "The consensus is that we first have to establish if the boys down the street are involved in any or all of the robberies. We've appointed three people here to search the public record files in the local newspaper to see if any of the boy's names appear under records of arrest. They will get that information to us next week. If the boys are involved, I will personally meet with our neighbor, the commissioner, and ask for his help. If he is willing to help, we will be well on the way to solving our problems. If not, we will decide what actions we can take from that point on. The secondary issue is the subdivision fee. We have decided that until we can get some closure on whether the boys are actually involved, we will start a campaign to get our property owners to pay their fees. We have a committee of five who will report to us next week on the steps they will take to get that campaign started. Now, suppose we do not establish that the neighborhood boys are not involved, then it will be extra important to get this Neighborhood Crime Watch under way. One of us has agreed to arrange to have a police representative here next week to get the project started."

Tom closed the meeting by expressing his appreciation for the willingness that almost everyone expressed for working together. He felt optimistic and was greatly relieved that these people were committed to solving their mutual concerns. He left the clubhouse that night very happy that his family had chosen to live in Lakeside View Estates.

The Case of Beverly Jacoby

The Problem

Sally Nauman decided to take the steps up the three flights of stairs to Beverly Jacoby's office. The walk would help take her mind off of the tension she and Beverly had been under during the past several days. She had hated it 3 days ago when she had sprung the news on Beverly that most of the nurses were refusing to attend the weekend seminar that had been planned for the last two months. That day, she had watched Beverly nearly come apart. Bev's immediate reaction was to want to fire Georgia Parker, the Licensed Practical Nurse (*LPN*) who undoubtedly had been inciting everybody else. Sally was able to restrain Bev, at least temporarily, until both of them could have a chance to talk with one of the management consultants from Chelsney, Blake, and Morrison.

Sally arrived in Bev's office just as Dr. Lawrence Morrison was escorted in by the receptionist. Both Sally and Bev had attended a workshop on effective leadership presented by Dr. Morrison and had retained his business card in the event that a situation like this one would ever come up.

"I understand from our phone conversation, Bev," Dr. Morrison said, "that your supervising nurses are refusing to attend the weekend workshop and that—as the Director of Nursing—you are at a loss as to how to handle the situation." Dr. Morrison opened a pocket notebook and set it on the table. "Can you fill me in a bit more on the situation and what's gone on up until now?"

Sally looked over at Bev and wondered if she could tell him what was at the heart of the situation. As Bev's assistant director, Sally knew the entire chain of events firsthand. As Bev's closest friend, she also knew how vulnerable Bev had been feeling.

Bev sipped her coffee and then gently put the cup down in front of her. "Dr. Morrison, Sally and I are in charge of dispensing nurses for home health care. The Home Health Care division is one part of the Fairchild Medical Group, which is a privately owned complex of medical services. Another division within the Fairchild organization is Patient Relations. The personnel in Patient Relations are the ones who are contacted by the referring physicians. They make the initial visit to the patient's home or residential treatment facility."

"Are there problems between your two divisions?" Dr. Morrison asked.

"That's putting it mildly," Bev replied. "The PR people make the treatment plan in accordance with the physician's orders, but they make promises that we simply cannot keep. You see, they don't actually treat the patients. We do that. They are supposed to determine what the patient's treatment needs are going to be and then give us a detailed report that we can follow up with. Our job is to assign one of our nurses to the case who will then dispense the treatment according to the plan."

"Sounds reasonable so far," Morrison said.

"So far it is," Bev remarked. "The problem comes in when the PR people write treatment plans that are beyond our abilities to carry out. You see, we feel that they are trying to make Fairchild look good to the physicians so the referrals will keep coming in. So they write up treatment plans for round-the-clock nursing care, to be provided by nurses specialized in whatever condition the patient suffers from. I think that if someone were to look into this whole thing from a legal side, Fairchild could be sued."

"We've even considered talking to the company lawyer," Sally added. "The problem is that some of our nurses are specialists, so the PR people really aren't out and out lying. But they create havoc for us because when our inexperienced LPNs arrive and the patient was expecting a cardiac nurse, the patient has a fit, or his family has a fit, and guess who gets the brunt of it?"

"The poor LPN," Dr. Morrison replied sympathetically.

"Exactly," Bev confirmed. "Our nurses get all the blame for promises they had nothing to do with. They are harassed, ridiculed, and a lot of times treated more like housemaids than professional nurses. What complicates matters is that many of them have yelled back at the patients or their families. Some of them have even walked out. You can imagine how PR feels about us when they get complaints from irate families or, worse yet, from physicians who threaten to cut off referrals."

"Have you tried going to your administrator," Morrison inquired, "so that you and the PR people can resolve the conflict through some sort of mediation?"

"PR refuses to sit down with us," Sally responded. "They see themselves as the sales force for Fairchild and claim that it is up to us to keep the customers happy after the sale has been closed."

"And what does Administration say?" Morrison asked.

"They're kind of giving us a backstabbing support," Bev answered. "You see, they won't force PR to change its policies which makes life miserable for us. But they have been willing to buy us off so that we will stop our complaining."

"How so?" Morrison questioned.

Sally replied, "Dr. Morrison, before Bev took over as the Director of Nursing about six months ago, we worked under a real dictator. The problelms in PR were still there, but under Virginia Murphy, you either put up or shut up. If you didn't like the guff the patients would give you, you could quit. Most people stayed on though because they knew Murphy would try to blackball them for any further work as a nurse. Fairchild brought Bev on right after Murphy retired. I think part of all this is my fault because after telling Bev all about Old lady Murphy, she went to the other extreme."

"Sally, don't go blaming yourself," Bev said reassuringly. "It is true, Dr. Morrison, that I did go to the other extreme. I guess I am probably too lenient with the nurses. Now they're getting away with murder. They are late to their assignments, they're rude to the patients, and they've become excessively demanding. In the last few weeks, they have banded together and insisted that the only way that they'll continue to put up with the situation is if they get more money. They are already the highest paid nurses in the community.

"Last week I went to Administration and presented their case for more money. Our CEO conditionally agreed, with the stipulation that any further complaints would not go beyond the Director of Nursing. So they got more money, they're still complaining, and I've sold my soul. Administration has refused to listen to me any further. I am literally caught in the middle.

"Now what is this business about a seminar?" Dr. Morrison inquired.

"Two months ago," Sally answered, "Bev and I came up with the idea that perhaps we could have a workshop that could teach our nurses how to handle the tirades they face when they walk into the patient's setting. After all, the problems are created by the PR people. Our nurses are getting the anger that is really meant for PR, not for them. So we figured that our nurses could be trained to calm the patient down and solve whatever problems they could right then and there. In that way, the nurse could then go about giving the patient the best treatment possible and, as a result, Fairchild's good name could be preserved."

"And," Dr. Morrison said and then paused.

"And," Bev continued, "at the time all of our nurses agreed that a workshop would be a good idea. We planned to get away over a weekend at a local retreat facility so that we could combine the workshop with a nice relaxing time. Up until the last couple of weeks, the plans were proceeding on schedule. Then some of the nurses started pressuring me for more money. I resisted initially, which I'm sure caused some resentment. By the time I was able to get Administration to agree to a blanket raise, two or three of the nurses started trying to convince everyone else not to give up their weekend for the workshop. So, right now as it stands, only three people out of the twenty that we have paid for plan to attend. I have done a complete turnaround as far as the way I have related to them. Unless they show up at the retreat center at 9:00 A.M. on Friday morning and stay clear through until Sunday noon, they will not have a job to come back to on Monday morning. When Virginia Murphy treated them like that, she got results."

"Yes, but you're not Virginia Murphy!" Sally protested to Bev. "You are overreacting to the whole mess, and by doing something stupid like this you're making everything worse."

Beverly looked unhappy. "You see, Dr. Morrison, now even Sally and I are fighting. I simply don't know what to do. I've got a workshop coming up in less than 24 hours that will cost the firm over $3000 whether or not we go through with it. Only three people said they would attend and I have threatened everybody else with their job. On top of all of that, my CEO refuses to help me any further. All I can hope for now is that somehow you can advise me how to take control of this situation."

The Solution

The Relationship Life Cycle.   Beverly and her staff of nurses are in the stage of the relationship life cycle called "eroded commitment." The jolts have accumulated over several months. The tension has reached the point of explosion. Since the nurses no longer feel a sense of commitment to Beverly, the only way she believes she can control them is through the force of an ultimatum. Looking back through the concepts in the relationship life cycle, Beverly really never did establish interpersonal credibility with her staff. Her superiors recognized her as an authority based on her technical competence as a nurse. However, the organization itself restricted her powers. As such, she was unable to correct the root cause of the difficulties her staff faced—namely, the confusion and resentment of the home health patients toward Beverly's personnel when they arrived to care for them. Beverly's attempts to support her staff by working to resolve the problem with the Patient Relations department were frustrated by her superiors. Her attempts to appease her staff by getting them more money represented a "bandaid" solution. The problem never went away. Her technical skills as a nurse simply had not prepared her to deal with the interpersonal problems she experienced on all fronts—with her superiors, her peers in the other department, and her subordinates.

We can see that Beverly needs to deal with the jolts that have affected her and her nurses. As of now, there is significant instability on her work team. We might ask why she does not go back to her superiors or pursue a resolution with her peers in Patient Relations? But this is no option, because she feels isolated from everyone. Aside from the support she has from her friend Sally, she is totally alone. Her first step in resolving the problem between her division, Patient Relations, and Administration is to resolve the specific problem within her own work team—that is, her lack of interpersonal credibility. There is no agreement to work together in solving the problem. Instead, there have been ultimatums and threats on both sides. The nurses want more money, while Beverly threatens to fire them if they don't attend the seminar. Beverly needs instead to find a way to integrate them toward a common goal: to find some way to solve this problem together as a work team. Once they have become integrated, Beverly can go to her superiors as a representative of her group. Currently, she is an adversary.

The behavior operating system. The problems between the Patient Relations division and the Home Health Care division of the Fairchild medical group have triggered the superegos of nearly everyone involved. Recall that as physical and emotional pressures build, the capacity to reason weakens. And when the brain's resources for thinking collapse, the brain's systems for self-protection go into operation. Planning and forethought are replaced by impulsive action and reaction.

The refusal by the nurses to attend the seminar "superego triggered" Beverly. Her superego flooded her ego with anxiety, which she experienced in terms of a sense of helplessness, a challenge to her authority, an assault to her dignity, and a rejection of her worthiness as a person. Her ego, already strained from the long-lasting complications of this problem, collapsed under the pressure. She could no longer think through what reasonable options were available. Her id, perceiving that she felt a great deal of emotional pain, came on line in an attempt to restore her equilibrium. We know that the id impulsively discharges aggressive behavior as it tries to remove the source of the pain: in this case, Beverly threatened to fire any nurse who did not attend the seminar.

The consultant that Beverly and Sally called in advised them to call a meeting that afternoon with the nursing staff. Since the nurses were all in the office that afternoon, Beverly could have her secretary direct them to report to the conference room at 1 o'clock for an update on the weekend seminar.

THE CONFRONTATION

"It's 1:05," Beverly said. "All but one of us is here, so we'll get started. First of all, I want you to know that none of you will lose your job if you don't come to the seminar. I came on a little heavy handed when I threatened to fire anyone who didn't attend. "You know, I can't remember a time in my life when I have been so frustrated with anything. It seems like you and I are caught in the middle of a problem that we didn't cause. The company won't give us a way to solve it and so we've had to take the brunt of it all this time. When I came to you all before and asked you what would help, you thought getting more money would make it easier. Administration agreed, but only after getting me to promise that I wouldn't come back to them about the problem anymore. I think we can all agree that the money hasn't helped anything. The patients still get upset when we show up instead of the types of nurses PR promised them. "A couple of months ago, I thought we all agreed that this seminar on how to handle angry patients would help us. Then, all of a sudden when a bunch of you refused to come, I was totally shocked. I really thought we found a way to handle the problem, and then it all broke down within a matter of hours. My frustration got the better of me and I started making threats. I was wrong to come on that way. After everything that's happened, we still have the problem. Whether or not we have the seminar this weekend, we still have to go into the patients' homes on Monday. They're still going to be upset, and we still will not have solved the problem.

"I think we should put our heads together and figure out what to do. It would really help me to understand what went wrong as far as the seminar is concerned."

Beverly waited.

The Reply

"Bev, you sort of forced us into the idea of a weekend seminar," June Wilcox said. "No one really wanted to give up their free time to come back to work, not to mention having to stay overnight. At first, the thought of getting away for a weekend with just us girls sounded marvelous. But then we all realized that the laundry would pile up, no one at home would have done the dishes, the house would be a mess, and all of that would be waiting for us to play catch-up that whole next week. It just wasn't fair to expect us to do all that."

"Besides that," Glenda Mason said, "why should we have to solve the problem? We think that you should go back to Administration and get them to straighten out the people in Patient Relations. Why should we have to pay for their mistakes? Or maybe they should come to the seminar, too."

"Bev, it's not that we have anything against you personally," Martha Compton told her. "You are usually a very nice person to work for. You're certainly an improvement over Virginia Murphy. But at least we knew the rules with her, you know. She was very consistent. If we didn't follow her laws, we were out. She actually fired a whole bunch of people. Bev, we're never sure with you."

Feedback

"Never sure?" Bev reflected. "I'm not really clear on what you mean. Could you help me with that?"

The Reply

"One day you're all peaches and cream," Martha told her. "The next day, you threaten to fire us. It's hard to know what to expect you to do or say from day to day."

"Maybe if we could have the seminar during the week, it would work out better," Phyllis McCormack suggested. "Then we wouldn't have to leave our families for the weekend."

"The seminar is missing the boat," protested Anna Wheeler. "We have to do something about those idiots in PR. They're the ones who are screwing it up for all of us. I'm telling you, if we don't get them to stop misrepresenting us, some angry family is going to sue."

SUMMARY

"Let me kind of sum up what I think everybody is saying," Beverly said. "First of all, we would all be a lot better off if I didn't schedule any overnight weekend seminars for us. In fact, Saturday and Sunday meetings even cause problems because they interfere with your needs at home. Second of all, I haven't really been consistent in what I've wanted from you. That's been confusing for you and, as a result, many of you have been feeling that I haven't really known what I've been talking about and that I wouldn't be able to get us out of this mess no matter what I wanted us to do. The third thing is that regardless of what we all decide, the problem is not going to change until we get Administration to put some pressure on Patient Relations. Many of you are nodding your heads. Have I missed anything? No, okay."

THE DECISION

"Now, there have been a lot of good suggestions about what we should do, so far. I think many of them are workable. The thing I'm most concerned about right now is the money our department will lose if we cancel the seminar. We have given a nonrefundable fee of $3000 to the training firm for the program this weekend. If we cancel, we lose the money. I still believe that we all could get a lot out of it. Remember, the program is supposed to help us learn some ways to help calm down the patients and their families so we can get them to accept our nursing care. That seems worthwhile to me.

"So, we are going to hold the seminar. I will not require you to attend. I think that many of you will. Those of you who want or need to can certainly feel free to leave after the afternoon sessions are over on Saturday. Come back on Sunday morning if you can.

"Instead of the role play exercises that the trainers have worked up for us to go through on Sunday morning, I have a different idea. I would like us to continue our discussion that we have started today. We care about the organization and we care about the patients. We can figure out a way to deal with this problem if we do it together."

THE REPLY

"You would be willing to go back to administration at some point?" Anna Wheeler asked with determination.

Summary and Decision

"Absolutely," Beverly said with commitment. "But not without the support of my staff, all of you. It is not fair that you've had to cover up for what Patient Relations has done. I'm sure they have their side of the story, but until we know what it is, we shouldn't have to condone what they are doing at our expense.

"I know I'm feeling better about all of this," Beverly continued. "I would like you to be there tomorrow. Those of you who feel like they can stay tomorrow night and Saturday night, fine. We've got a lot of fun things planned that your husbands probably wouldn't approve of if they knew. If you do decide to go home, it's okay. I don't want us to get sidetracked into who can be more stubborn. The important thing is for us to start working together. I'd like you to help me get us started."

The Case of Jerry Williams

The Problem

The neighbor's dog had been barking for what seemed like hours. Since Jerry Williams had been promoted to upper management in the prestigious accounting firm of Marks, Kensington & Beasley, he had been having trouble sleeping anyway. One of the firm's partners, John Kensington, had staunchly opposed his promotion. The other two partners, Roger Marks and Steven Beasley, had assured Jerry that they would get Kensington to approve, but they weren't successful. There was no way that Kensington could actually block Jerry's promotion. The corporate bylaws stipulated that advancement within the company required affirmative votes from only two out of the three partners. Surely, the promotion was deserved. After all, a great deal of the firm's financial stability during the last several quarters stemmed from his close scrutiny of the corporate books. Even so, Kensington was making his life miserable.

Jerry wondered if this man perceived some weakness in him that the other partners overlooked. He was even beginning to question himself and, lately, his frequent periods of self-doubt were disturbing his sleep. Last night, he had been able to fall asleep all right, but the neighbor's barking dog woke him up.

He had thought about calling next door, but he knew he might end up saying something he'd later regret. At 2:30 A.M. he got up out of bed, put on a robe, went to the bathroom, and then made sure each of the kids was covered. He gently tugged at Aaron to try to get him to stop grinding his teeth. He'd stop for a while and then start up again. It was a toss up for Jerry as to which was more annoying, the damn dog's howling or Aaron's teeth grinding. He tried to shut out both sounds by thinking about something else, but that made matters worse by getting caught up in worries about Kensington and the office. Alice interrupted his thoughts briefly when she told him to stop moving around in bed so much.

When the alarm went off at 6:45, he remembered having last looked at the clock at 4:30. His head hurt, his back ached, and he felt like he was hung over. He hit the snooze button and didn't get out of bed for another 35 minutes. The executive meeting was scheduled for 8:30 this morning instead of its usual time on Wednesday at 9 o'clock. Jerry didn't know how he'd push his way through the morning traffic to get there on time. John Kensington took personal offense when anyone walked in late.

"Alice, where are my white shirts?"

Alice called up the steps in an irritated tone of voice, "I told you they're still in the dirty clothes hamper. I asked you if you needed them today and you said 'no.'"

"God darn it, Alice, that was before I knew the executive meeting was changed. I need a white shirt for it and I need it now."

"Well, how in heck am I supposed to know these things unless you tell me. You expect me to read your mind? You told me you didn't need them."

Jerry settled for a long-sleeve blue shirt that he laid out on the bed before dashing into the shower. He heard Alice call up again asking him what he wanted for breakfast. "Just coffee," he yelled back down. "I won't have time for anything else."

It was 8:10 when he reached for his coffee at the breakfast table. "Fine example you set for your children, running out of here on an empty stomach," Alice said accusingly.

"Don't start with me, Alice," Jerry snapped back. I didn't sleep half the night, I've got this damn meeting with Kensington in 15 minutes that I'm never going to make on time. I don't need you rambling on like your mother right now." She picked up the paper as if she were going to throw it, but he was out the front door before he knew if she really would.

The drive to work usually took 10 minutes, but traffic on the crosstown highway was backed up so Jerry doubted that he would make it on time. Still, he had to try. He saw a clearing in the right access lane and started to cut in front of an oncoming car.

The driver got upset, pounded on his horn, and purposely sped up trying to keep Jerry from getting into the space. He floored his car and was able to weave in before the other driver cut him off.

Jerry felt like slamming on his brakes to force the idiot to ram him from behind. In the meantime, he accelerated again trying to work his way into the line of traffic on the highway. He tried to stay calm, but he could feel his heart racing from his intolerance of all these jackass people. "I'd like to get my hands on the son-of-a-gun who's holding up all this traffic," he heard himself saying out loud. "Why in the hell can't people use their heads when they drive." At that point, he had broken out in a cold sweat and was pounding his fist against the wheel.

It was 8:40 when he approached the conference room. He took out a handkerchief and patted his forehead. His hair fell down across this eyebrow and he threw his head back trying to force it back into place. "Damn Alice for breaking the hair-styling dryer," he thought angrily as he turned the knob on the huge oak door.

Jerry smiled politely at John Kensington. Kensington nodded his head slightly in reply, picked up his glasses from the table, put them on so that they rested somewhat forward on the bridge of his nose, and said, "Now, perhaps we can begin."

The meeting did not go well. Kensington questioned several conclusions that Jerry had reached in his report. The division that he had just taken over recently lost several prominent accounts.

"Jerry, I don't understand where your head is man," Kensington barked. "You can't go giving away the firm's services like this. People expect to pay for quality. Hell, why don't you just take out an ad in the newspaper with 50-percent-off coupons?

"John, this proposal came from our marketing division," Jerry said in his own behalf.

"Don't hand me that," Kensington retorted. "You signed the damn thing. At least you could have proofread it." He flipped through the document showing Jerry several pages that he had marked in red. Then he shoved the proposal across the table. "Looks like you've got your work cut out for you as a manager, doesn't it boy?" Kensington looked down at his agenda. "All right, what other bright ideas do we have to talk about today? Let's get on with it."

Jerry was mortified and humiliated. His heart was racing, and he sensed that his skin had lost all color. As soon as the meeting was over, he stormed into the secretarial pool and threw the proposal on Theresa Sanchez's desk.

"You told me you proofread this damn thing," he yelled.

"I did," Theresa said meekly.

"Well, these aren't gold stars," Jerry said as he flipped through the pages. "Kensington caught these."

"Oh my God, I'm sorry Mr. Williams," Theresa said, obviously ashamed for her oversights.

"I'm sorry," Jerry said mimicking her. "You made me look like a complete idiot to the head of this company. What the hell were you doing when you were supposed to be proofing this, huh? Flirting around with one of those dudes who are always calling you on the office phones? Maybe if you'd stay the hell away from them dudes of yours you could concentrate on your work. For Christ's sake, Theresa, its going to take me months to shake this off." He ripped the proposal in half, threw it down at her typewriter, and abruptly left the room.

Janet, Theresa's co-worker, brought her a box of tissues. "You know, Theresa, you could get him on discrimination for that. EEOC wants to know about people like him. He had no right to talk to you like that."

Theresa reached for the tissues and cried almost inaudibly at her desk for several minutes. She looked down the hall toward her supervisor's office, hesitated momentarily, then slowly walked toward it.

About an hour later, Jerry's secretary notified him that Mr. Kensington was calling. "Shall I put the call through, Mr. Williams?"

"Yes, of course," Jerry said. His heart started racing again. He took a deep breath in hopes that he could cover up the quivering that would undoubtedly be in his voice. The phone rang once and Jerry picked it up.

"Yes John, this is Jerry."

"Get in my office right now," Kensington ordered and then hung up abruptly.

The Solution

The Relationship Life Cycle.   This case study is about an accountant who reached a position of management prematurely. The story focuses on Jerry's anxieties, which all seem to revolve around John Kensington, the firm's third partner who did not support Jerry's rise to the top. Although Jerry could clearly benefit from a course in stress management, the obstacles standing between his current technical competence and the skills he would need to become a competent manager are clearly blocking his success. Kensington recognizes this fact. Apparently the firm's other two partners, Marks and Beasley, do not. In other words, the relationship between Jerry and Kensington never went past the credibility stage. Kensington views Jerry as lacking the directive skills for management. Even before Jerry made incriminating remarks to the secretary, his poor skills in organization and presentation resulted in critical comments from Kensington. Since Jerry never established credibility with Kensington, we cannot actually consider that there had been a jolt between them. In order for a jolt to occur, the members of the relationship had to have experienced stability in their work functions. Such stability had never occurred between this manager and this executive.

The behavior operating system.   Despite the fact that we cannot view the conflicts in this story as true jolts, we can recognize an abundance of superego triggers. Jerry seemed plagued by them—including the argument with his wife, the difficulties he experienced in traffic, and the criticism from Kensington. Kensington himself was "superego triggered" by Jerry—first by the incomplete and inaccurate reports and second by the legal complications that Jerry's comments to the secretary could pose to the company. Indeed, these very comments clearly were a superego trigger for Theresa. Her actions, while perhaps not impulsive, were driven by a need to settle the score with Jerry.

Overall, the story illustrates the situation of a person who is placed in a management position without having developed the necessary directive skills; such a person's threshold for pressure will cave in, giving way to impulsive behavior. If Jerry has any chance to succeed as a manager, he must first establish credibility with his superiors, namely, Kensington. Unfortunately, it may be too late because of Jerry's conduct with Theresa. His impulsive remarks reflected a lack of emotional stability and raised serious questions in Kensington's mind about Jerry's ethical credibility.

Even though this story focused on Jerry, the person in the leadership role was clearly Kensington. He was responsible for making company decisions, directing the company's resources, and representing the company's image. It is his responsibility to confront Jerry regarding the difficulties he posed to the company's welfare.

CONFRONTATION

"Come in, Jerry. Sit down right here in front of my desk," Kensington told him. His voice was surprisingly calm. "You made a statement to Theresa Sanchez in the secretarial pool. According to my notes, you accused her of flirting with 'dudes,' and you yelled profanity at her. Her supervisor told me that Theresa is considering filing a formal complaint with the EEOC. This company could be in serious trouble because of your statements. We could lose a great deal of time, even more money, and it could wreck our good name in the community. Besides all that, we might lose a damn good secretary. Now, I have to admit, the thought of firing you crossed my mind more than once before this happened. I frankly don't think you're cut out for management. At this point, the only thing that's holding me back is your good standing with Marks and Beasley. I don't know what you did to sell them, but they are still going to bat for you. As a favor to them, I agreed to give you an opportunity to present your side."

THE REPLY

"John, I would like another chance," Jerry said. "I haven't gotten off to a very good start in management. Oh, not only here at the company, but my home life has been a wreck too. I think the pressure of trying to convince you that I can do it has really been getting to me. I've taken it out on my wife, I haven't been sleeping, I've let mistakes get past me in my reports, and I said some things to Theresa without thinking. I guess that proves to me that I could never make a very good manager."

LISTENING WITH A DOOR OPENER

"Never make a very good manager," Kensington reflected." I'm not sure what you mean by that."

THE REPLY

Jerry thought for a moment and then said, "I know what a manager is supposed to do. Every college kid who's ever taken a business course can tell you that. I used to help the guys in my fraternity study the principles for planning, organizing, and making control adjustments. Somehow I can't seem to get it all together now. When I try, I get frustrated and the pressure gets to me."

SUMMARY

"Then as you see it, you have the book knowledge," Kensington stated. "The problem is that you don't know how to make it all work on the job. When you've tried, you get all caught up in your own frustrations. Then you take it out on people like your wife and your secretary, and yourself."

THE REPLY

"That's it," Jerry admitted. "I'm a damn good accountant. It's not that I can't handle pressure. My old job had more than its fair share of stress. Seems like I was more ready for that though when I got into my first job in accounting than how I'm doing now in management."

THE DECISION

"It may surprise you to hear me say this after what you've done today, Jerry, but you need to hear it anyway," Kensington said. "This company has not given you a fair chance to prove yourself. My two gung ho partners flung you into a management position before you were ready for it. I need to get on them myself for that. You need some help in moving from what you've been so good at, accounting, to what you may someday be good at, managing. Right now, there is a big gap between the two. It's a serious gap. On the one hand, you have done things as an accountant that have made us a great deal of money. On the other hand, you've done things as a manager that could cost us a great deal of money.

"As of right now, I am relieving you of all your responsibilities as a manager. In a few minutes, I am going to ask Theresa to come in here. Her supervisor informed me that she would be willing to consider an apology as long as she didn't have to accept work from you anymore. I expect you to give her that apology. I will stay here in the office with you while you talk to her. Tomorrow morning, you will go back to your old job in accounting. Beginning next quarter, if you want it, you can begin attending our in-house management-training program. Good old Marks and Beasley think their people are too smart for our instructors. You have proven to them, once and for all I hope, that smarts just aren't enough to be an effective manager. Our trainers don't let go of you once you pass their classes. They follow you like a hawk until you convince them—and me for that matter—that you can make it outside of the classroom. Then and only then will you get saddled with the responsibilities of management. That's my decision, Jerry. Unless I'm wrong, I think that decision is going to help you sleep a lot better tonight."

SUMMARY

In this chapter, we have applied the skills from the entire book to three case studies. Tom Demerist, Beverly Jacoby, and John Kensington each served as leadership models in demonstrating the processes of confrontation, feedback, and decision making. The nature of each problem varied from case to case. Yet, the principles for approaching the solutions were remarkably consistent. Though people differ in countless ways, human behavior follows the laws of nature. When people succumb to superego triggers, they need to be desensitized from the superego. At that point, their ego will help them to redirect their mental energies from impulsive channels to rational thinking. The effective leader knows how to make it happen.

TOPICS FOR DISCUSSION

1. Reread the case study of Mike and Kathy from Chapter 2. Develop a set of solutions to their problem by applying the framework from the case studies in this chapter.

2. The case study in Chapter 3 involving Mrs. Collins and John Baker ended with Mrs. Collin's decision to fire John. Develop an alternate ending in which Mrs. Collins confronts John, considers his reply, provides feedback, and arrives at a mutually advantageous solution.

3. Many people have experienced difficulty in working for a particular supervisor or manager. Try to recall a situation in which you were involved that did not end well. How might that situation have been different if that supervisor or manager had used the principles in this book?

CHAPTER SEVEN
SUMMARY

OUTLINE

OVERVIEW
QUESTIONS AND ANSWERS
FINAL EXAMINATION

Success in business requires effective leadership. Without firm control and sound organization, companies face serious risks of business failure. For the majority of people, leadership does not come naturally. There are many instances in which ill-prepared individuals suddenly become saddled with the responsibilities of leadership.

Many businesses simply do not recognize the relationship between their levels of productivity and the competence levels of their leaders. Companies often promote personnel to positions of leadership without first establishing whether or not such people are sufficiently qualified to take on leadership roles. The concept of leadership is typically regarded as a self-encompassing skill that can be quickly learned rather than as a field of study that requires a great deal of theoretical and practical assimilation. It is not at all uncommon for companies to send its newly promoted supervisors and managers to attend brief seminars on leadership just as casually as they would send them to seminars on time management or effective speaking. Unfortunately, success in leadership does not lend itself to abbreviated training. Attempts to mold neophyte leaders to the molds of "one shot" leadership programs are often disappointing and sometimes disasterous.

A *leader* was defined as an individual who has the authority to decide, direct, and represent the objectives and functions of an organization. Leadership incorporates the functions of management, namely, the direction of the organization's resources, in order to accomplish objectives. Leadership goes beyond managment in its other functions. A leader is responsible for the organization itself. As its chief representative, the leader is held accountable and responsible for the welfare and the actions of the organization. The organization, of course, can vary significantly in size, scope, and complexity. Regardless, the leader shapes the direction, manages the activities, and represents the policies and products as the person who has charge of the organization as a whole and integrated entity.

Becoming recognized as an authority is nearly always a prerequisite for gaining a position in leadership. This recognition stems from the belief by certain groups of people in the individual's competence to perform the leadership roles. A leader can establish technical credibility by convincing an organization that she is technically competent to perform the work tasks that the organization expects of her. If she is successful, the organization recognizes her as an authority whose credibility is rooted in her technical competence. Subsequently, the organization turns over to her the power to direct its resources so that its objectives can be accomplished. Or, a leader can establish that he has ethical credibility by convincing representative members of society that he is someone who will not intentionally seek to satisfy himself at the expense of other people. If he is successful, society will permit the leader to go on about the business of directing human resources to accomplish the desired objectives. In addition to technical and ethical forms of credibility, a leader can be recognized as an authority through interpersonal credibility. That is, if he is able to convince his prospective followers that he can help them get what they want, they will give the leader powers by which he can direct their behaviors.

If structured training is related to effective leadership, its success would very likely depend upon some mixture of theory and practice. This book has focused on one component of the theory-practice mix, namely, a leader's relationships with people.

Working relationships follow a logical sequence in terms of how they begin, function, and in some cases, stumble and disintegrate. The unsuccessful relationship follows a sequence of events marked by accumulating tensions over unresolved conflicts that end in the termination of the relationship. The successful relationship follows a cycle through which conflicts are confronted and resolved so that the productive functions of the relationship are maintained.

Conflict between people is completely normal. It is a natural way through which individual differences are expressed. People never stay the same. As such, their needs for their life also change. For a working relationship to remain functional, it has to accommodate the changes that its members experience. Conflict arises between the members when they change in ways that threaten one another. One member perceives that the other member may be trying to hurt him or her in some way. This perception triggers anxiety. The natural reaction is to try to defend oneself against what feels like an attack. Often the defense takes the form of a counterattack. The stage is then set to intensify the conflict rather than to see it resolved.

The ability to preserve order within the work team requires the leader to implement the various forms of power with which she has been entrusted. Her use of power must be tempered with reason, patience, and prudent judgment. The knowledge of how human temperament maintains the body's internal balance alerts her to her own areas of physiological and emotional vulnerability. She knows all too well that the daily pressures that constantly confront her can all too easily trigger impulsive reactions that can seriously jeopardize the company's ability to meet its objectives. Her obligation as a company leader is to implement leadership functions with judicious rather than impulsive power. Furthermore, this knowledge prepares her to redirect the anxieties and frustrations among her subordinates into productive rather than destructive channels.

Intelligence alone cannot assure that decisions in leadership will be made on a rational basis. However, the knowledge that tensions and anxieties can disable the process of rational thinking can significantly contribute to emotional stability in the leadership role. Events that cause people to feel anxious and threatened were defined as *superego triggers*. How we deal with a superego trigger will determine the nature of our actions. If the rational dimension of our mental framework, the ego, has been operating under physical or emotional strain, it will likely collapse under the pressure of the anxieties. The id will subsequently perceive the existing anxieties as a threat to our internal balance (homeostasis) and will attempt to neutralize that threat by steering bodily energies into impulsive and aggressive behaviors. However, if the ego is capable of efficient operations, it can disperse the anxieties into channels of clear thinking. Actions will then by guided by the process of reason and sound judgment.

According to many experts the effective leader has developed the knowledge, skills, and temperament for working with people. The actual traits of the leader's personality appear to be less important than the ways the leader actually treats the people who follow. The knowledge includes an understanding of factors that determine the "hows" and "whys" of typical human behavior. The procedural guidelines in this book have provided a means through which the leader can redirect human behavior from impulsive and self-serving actions into productive channels that can benefit the worker as well as the organization.

QUESTIONS AND ANSWERS

Q: *I don't understand what learning about the personality has to do with leadership. Is it really necessary?*

A: Research has not established exactly what type of training is necessary for effective leadership. The results of scientific investigations in the area of leadership have largely been based on what is called empirical evidence, that is, the process of discovering truth by experience. This experience has confirmed that competence in leadership depends upon an ability to get along with people—to be both firm and flexible as well as empathic and objective. These qualities are important because people are dynamic, that is, their behaviors change at hair-raising speeds. The dynamic nature of human behavior becomes quite clear when one understands the way the human personality is programmed for the purpose of self-protection. The personality orders impulsive action when anxiety threatens internal harmony and emotional stability. Reason gives way to irrational thinking. Productive behavior is soon replaced by dysfunctional performance. The leader who understands the utility of this neurological programming can often restore rational behavior by reducing the anxiety. The knowledge of these personality functions can thereby guide the leader's actions through a structured framework that remains constant and stable during the most challenging and pressuring circumstances.

Q: *Much of the theoretical foundation on which this training model is based relates to the work of Freud. Hasn't modern day science rejected Freud's notions?*

A: It is important to recognize that this book focuses on only one aspect of Freud's principles. That aspect is the organization of the personality. Freud's writings also included a great deal of work in the area of psychopathology and the treatment of mental disorders. His contributions are regarded by many historical and contemporary scientists as the cornerstone of psychoanalytic psychotherapy. There are many mental health practitioners and philosophers who do question the validity of psychoanalytic methods as well as the presumptions underlying their procedures. However, very few scientists argue about the precision and accuracy by which the concept of the id, ego, and superego explain the major functions of human personality. In fact, the twentieth century writings of the neurologist Papez have provided significant evidence that structures within the human personality do actually function in a manner that is highly consistent with Freud's descriptions (Papez, 1937). Of course, this evidence should come as little surprise since Freud himself was a neurologist (McKean, 1985).

Q: *Since the concepts in this book incorporate methods from psychotherapy, could I possibly do more harm than good in trying to use them?*

A: The model in the book is directed towards use with people who are capable of normal ego functions. The types of strain and pressure that are typical of business settings often trigger superego anxiety and subsequent outbursts from the id component of the personality. The methods in this book are designed to reduce that anxiety and promote harmless rather than destructive ventilation of id energies. In other words, by learning how to apply these methods both to yourself and to your subordinates, you are helping the ego to better do its job—to preserve order. As such, there is little if any risk of causing harm to anyone. However, if the subordinate's id continues to compromise stability on the work team after two or three attempts at trying to desensitize his superego, you have probably reached the limits of your skills. At that point, you must take action to prevent further disruption by referring the subordinate for psychological counseling or medical consultation.

Q: *Most of my subordinates are older than I am and resent that I have power over them. How can I handle their resistance to my authority?*

A: Awkward as the situation may be, you must keep in mind that your company is paying you to function in a position of leadership. Whether or not your older subordinates like it is secondary to the fact that you are in an executive role. They are not. Their resistance can be regarded as an indication that your age has served as a superego trigger. Their egos have been flooded with anxiety. Instead of repressing that anxiety or attempting to integrate it into productive work, they have allowed their egos to shut down. Subsequently, their id responds to the anxiety as a source of pain. The pain must be eliminated in order to restore their own internal stability. How do they attempt to relieve the pain? By overtly and covertly expressing resentment toward you.

How can you handle the resistance to your direction? First of all, recognize that you have not established interpersonal credibility with them. Remember Beverly Jacoby? Through a combination of confrontation and superego desensitizers, you can communicate your expectations to them and then give them ample opportunities to ventilate their feelings. Use door openers, quiet time, acknowledgements, paraphrases, and summaries. In general, retain your power base while you support their needs to feel important.

Q: *Suppose I have a personality conflict with one of my subordinates. As a leader, will I be expected to like and be liked by all of my subordinates?*

A: Interpersonal credibility is an absolute necessity for a leader to influence and motivate the members of the work team. However, interpersonal credibility has more to do with fairness than it does personality. Through the operations of your ego, you can structure the framework by which conflicts can be openly discussed and differences resolved. In the event that you implement a decision with which one or more subordinates disagree, you can give them ample opportunities to express their concerns or grievances. As long as you clearly communicate your expectations to your subordinates and allow them to communicate their reactions back to you, stability within the work team can usually be maintained.

The reason that you can effectively maintain stability is because you are in a position of power; your subordinates are not. However, your power cannot control the personal feelings that your subordinates have toward you. Interpersonal credibility is not the same as friendship. You can structure work performance; you cannot structure feelings. For whatever reason, despite your fairness and despite high levels of productivity and team morale, your subordinate may not regard you as a friend. In situations that exceed your authoritative limits, the subordinate may avoid and perhaps even be critical of you. Keep in mind that as long as the working relationship between you and this subordinate remains functional and stable, the personal differences between you is a secondary issue. If it interferes with the subordinate's work performance, you are within your executive boundaries to deal with it as a leader. If not, you must regard it as a personal issue. Deal with it as an individual, not as an authority. Remember, the direction of the work team is your job. Friendship is your pleasure. The two may intermingle, but they should never be regarded as one and the same.

Q: *Is it unethical to yell at your subordinates? Do you always have to be a nice guy?*

A: A leader who has established ethical credibility is still human. You will lose your temper, occasionally have one too many drinks, and think thoughts you would rather not make public. This book has not focused on leadership with respect to etiquette or morality. However, a leader who fails to scrutinize his or her words, actions, and deeds is simply not operating through the most effective part of his or her personality: the ego. As such a leader, your power will trigger defensive reactions among your followers. Stability within the work team will disintegrate, and consequently, you will have created more work for yourself since the preservation of stability is an essential part of your job.

In leadership terms, it is not a sin to yell at your subordinate. However, in economic terms, it may be very costly. The subordinate may retaliate against the assault through any number of overt or covert channels: attempts to turn other workers against you, withholding reasonable levels of enthusiasm and creativity, projecting anger toward you onto corporate clients, and so forth. In other words, yelling at the subordinate was your attempt to solve one problem. The act of doing so in effect created another problem. You alone must decide (ego) whether the cost of your outburst (id) merited the expense incurred by the subordinate's reaction (superego anxiety and retaliation from their id).

In many cases, prevailing levels of stress and tension will get the better of you. Your ego will cave in to superego anxiety and your id will impulsively break through. Hopefully, you will have enough reserves in your *ego* to express hostile feelings toward your subordinate's actions. For example:

> "John, I've about run out of patience waiting for you to finish the report. I feel like saying all sorts of things I don't really mean and I know I would later regret. I'm tired of putting aside the rest of my work until you get your part finished."

Try to get out as much energy from your id as you possibly can without attacking the other person's dignity and self-esteem. Let your voice convey your anger, frustration, worry, and disappointment. Use your words to clearly describe how the other person's actions have made your job extremely difficult for you to complete.

In the event that you do explode, so be it. It happened. Since you ventilated your aggression, you probably feel better and you can begin to calm down. As you do, remember that your job as a leader is to preserve order so that work functions can be maintained. In so doing, you must now deal with the consequences of your outburst by repairing the damage. Your id will begin to recede and energies will once again be made available to your ego. As your ego comes back on line, you will need to "superego desensitize" your subordinate. Since your id has just previously "superego triggered" him, his id will momentarily launch a defensive-aggressive response directed toward your superego.

Let him respond and get it out of his system. If you attempt to stop him with further superego triggers, you will only provoke him further; the intensity and frequency of the jolts will be compounded. Let him respond. When he does, do not interrupt him. Let him have his say. Use door openers to give him ample opportunity to ventilate even more. Your objective is to restore mental operations to his ego. Soothe his superego so that you can get his id off line as soon as you can. Once both of you are operating in your egos, you will have a much greater chance of resolving your differences to your mutual satisfaction.

The situation may have provoked such tension that a cool down period should be considered rather than to deal with the feelings on the spot. Sometimes time can provide enough emotional distance from the tense moments that both parties can approach their differences with clearer heads. Too much time, however, might allow the resentment to fester and harden beyond the point of resolution. Generally, differences that are not resolved within a few days intensify and become exaggerated beyond the events that actually occurred. These extended and ambiguous differences are the ones that erode commitment and all too soon lead to disintegration of the working relationship.

To summarize, a leader is only human. Of course, it is only normal for you as a leader to lose your temper once in a while. However, when losing your temper results in triggering a subordinate's superego, you must be prepared to deal with the consequences. The subordinate is also human. The subordinate's temperament is programmed to defend against a personal attack by some form of aggressive response. If you remain impulsive, the jolts will intensify and instability within the working relationship will be prolonged. You must access your own ego as quickly as possible so that your judicious powers can restore stability. If your own emotions prevent ego access, you should inform the subordinate that you can deal with the differences at a later time. When you both have calmed down after a brief period of time, you as leader can structure the discussion so that each side can express its concerns in a reasonable manner.

Q: *I don't always have the time to talk to my subordinates. Can't I just communicate through memos?*

A: The use of memos to announce policies carries the risk that they might be misinterpreted by whoever reads them. The misinterpretation can lead to the wrong action which could, of course, jeopardize your efforts to meet objectives. In addition, the reader might perceive that you are using the memo to criticize her for something she may have said or done. In either case, the use of a memo to communicate information does not allow communication to be bidirectional unless the reader chooses to send her own memo back to you. The result may lead to further ambiguity and misinterpretation. In other words, memos to announce policy or give direction may result in superego triggers in the receiver. A good rule of thumb is to send a memo only to summarize what has already been discussed and resolved. The memo should specifically state that its purpose is to confirm your understanding of a particular issue. If the receiver's understanding is different from what the memo has conveyed, he or she can so inform you. Any differences could then be resolved through further discussion, not through further memos.

Q: *Can I apply the principles in this book to my own personal life?*

A: To some extent, yes. However, your position as a leader comes with a predetermined degree of power. You can legitimately use this power in order to direct the work team over which you are responsible. This power structure does not exist within your personal relationships. Your power is essentially limited to whether or not you choose to remain in the relationship. With that power limitation as a qualification, you can apply the principles of human temperament and the relationship life cycle to your personal relationships.

Remember the case of Mike and Kathy? This couple had been married one year when Kathy, an attorney, had decided to create a special evening for herself and Mike as a celebration. Unfortunately, Mike was preoccupied with a business commitment. Upon coming home, he had Kathy's anger and disappointment to deal with. The case illustrated how both of these people became locked into id-superego struggles. Each triggered the other's superego, subsequently shutting down rational thinking and giving way to impulsive actions. The natural reaction was aggression as a defense—each trying to hurt the other.

The primary functions of a personal relationship are to provide companionship and pleasure. As long as each person satisfies the other in these ways, the relationship remains stable. However, when one person's needs conflict with the other's expectations, a jolt will result. The relationship will enter a period of instability. The partners no longer receive pleasure from one another. Subsequently, companionship brings pain.

With your knowledge of these concepts, you can help to restore stability to your relationship. Deal with the jolts as they come up. Don't let them pile up without talking them out.

Assume, for the moment, that your partner has "superego triggered" you. First of all, determine whether or not your own internal conditions have made you more vulnerable than usual. Are you tired or fatigued? Have you perhaps skipped a meal or neglected important nutrients in favor of quick sugars? Are you sluggish from insufficient physical activity? In other words, consider that the ease with which you can be superego triggered may be related to an internal imbalance. When you know for sure, help your partner understand that you are simply not feeling like yourself and that later would be a better time to resolve the problem at hand. Then suggest a time to talk about working out your differences.

Secondly, avoid flying off the handle in response to your partner's superego trigger. Recognize that your emotional temperature is climbing. Your ability to be aware of this anxiety is a sign that your ego is still operating. If you react defensively at this point, you will only superego trigger your partner and intensify their aggressive response. Instead, get some clarification. Use a door opener. Get them to talk about themselves. Find out what they want you to know. Remember, one of the main reasons that they have attacked you is to draw your attention to something that is bothering them. That something is coming from their id. It is physiologically charged. You cannot wish it away or pretend that it isn't there. If you instead help the partner express it, you will be enabling their id to discharge tension nondestructively. In so doing, the intensity of their superego triggers towards you will subside and they will begin to calm down. Then, so will you.

OTHER: I am sick and tired of cleaning up after you at dinner.

YOU: Go on . . .

OTHER: What do you mean, "go on." You know what I mean. It isn't fair that I have to work all day, then come home and cook dinner, and then have to clean everything up as well. It's about time you started pitching in. You know, sometimes I feel like you want me to treat you like a mother instead of a wife.

YOU: You mean it feels like I expect you to pick up after me like my mother told you she did?

OTHER: Yes, and I don't want to do it. It would make things a lot easier for me if we could somehow share chores at dinner.

YOU: I'm not sure what you mean when you say "share."

OTHER: Well, like you doing the dishes—maybe at least helping with the dishes. I know you're tired too. I don't mean to be taking out my frustrations on you. But it would mean so much to me if we could divide up the responsibilities. I guess that's why I've been so cranky lately.

YOU: Because everything's been kind of falling on your shoulders, not only at work but at home too.

OTHER: It really has.

YOU: You know, that makes a lot of sense to me. It's not that I think you should have to do more work than me. I feel terrible realizing that that's the way it's been working out around here. But you know, I was raised very differently. My mother did all the household chores. Right or wrong, my dad and all of us kids just left the table after we ate.

OTHER: But I'm not your mother. Besides, your mother didn't have to hold down a full-time job.

YOU: You're right, she didn't. I don't want you to be just like my mother. I love you, and I love the way you are. I'm willing to keep working at this, if you are. I'll wash the dishes tonight if you promise not to get mad if I break one. Maybe later we can talk about what we can do from now on. Okay?

OTHER: Okay. Come on. You wash and I'll dry. Here's the apron!

The key to working out jolts with a partner is to respond to their superego triggers with superego desensitizers. There is no doubt that this type of response is difficult. Your instinct will be to defend yourself by counterattacking. While the counterattack may not do any permanent harm, it will more than likely intensify the other person's anger toward you. As a result, the relationship will remain unstable. Each of you may feel like you have won the battle, but your victory may be one of loneliness and isolation.

Keep on talking to one another. Replace threats and vindictiveness with attempts to understand the other's needs. You do not have to give up what you want, nor do they. Instead of defending your position, spend a little more time understanding their's. Work to identify the issues that separate the two of you by listening, by clarifying, by summarizing, and by understanding. Once both sets of cards are on the table, then each of you can more rationally decide what changes, if any, must be made. Cooperation and compromise can sustain your relationship through the years of companionship.

You now know the tools that can make the companionship you both share a lifelong source of pleasure. As a leader in a business, your most potent resource is power. In your intimate personal relationships, your most potent resource is compromise.

Q: *How long can I expect to work at becoming an effective leader?*

A: Effective leadership is a process, not a product. Unfortunately, many consulting firms use subtle marketing campaigns that imply they can somehow turn supervisors and managers into leaders almost overnight. These types of campaigns misrepresent how people change as a result of learning. To expect that one can emerge from a "leadership" seminar with the competence to satisfy the real-life demands of a competitive business reflects an attitude that itself threatens the stability of that business.

Many people who complete the "quick-hitting" leadership seminars return to their work settings filled with high levels of confidence and motivation. However, within a few hours the reality of the daily strains break down the new methods that the students may have memorized from their brief and superficial exposure to them.

I cannot overemphasize that the lifeline of any business runs through its leadership. To expect that newly promoted supervisors and managers can be transformed into competent leaders by procedure-based training programs is inviting potentially disastrous consequences.

A great deal of leadership requires tact, flexibility, self-discipline, and courage. People must grow into these life skills. Leadership training should begin by teaching students about people: how we can be expected to function, how we relate with one another, and why we do what we do. Once the student is conceptually grounded in this basic understanding of human behavior, then—and only then—is it reasonable to expect him or her to apply this knowledge to directing that behavior.

Leadership is a lifelong process of learning and of adapting to the nuances of individual differences, the demands of the business, and the changes within oneself. You will always make some mistakes; occasionally, you will lose your temper; you will sometimes act more like an idiot than a seasoned leader; and you will more than infrequently wish you could have the luxury of being a subordinate instead of the person in charge. These reactions are normal. Remember, you are a person, not a machine. With a tremendous amount of persistence, self-confidence, self-determination, a burning desire to succeed, and a great deal of flexibility, you stand an excellent chance to take charge of the work team, to direct your company's human resources, and to enjoy the rank, privilege, and wealth of successful leadership.

FINAL EXAMINATION

1. Leadership is synonymous with which of the following:
    a. management
    b. dominance
    c. authority
    d. directing resources
    e. none of the above
2. Which of the following results will probably not occur simply by reading this book:
    a. the effective direction of a workforce
    b. the ability to differentiate leadership from management
    c. possess a framework for assessing effective leadership
    d. possess a knowledge base for applying leadership skills
    e. none of the above
3. Effective leadership will consider the human needs of the workforce without compromising the bottom-line needs of the organization.
    a. true
    b. false
4. The single most important task of leadership is to ensure that:
    a. the company meets its objectives.
    b. people are treated with dignity.
    c. a favorable public image is maintained.
    d. the company makes a profit.
    e. none of the above.
5. The license to use power stems from a leader's authority:
    a. true
    b. false
6. Intimidation is a form of authority.
    a. true
    b. false
7. Participants in most leadership seminars can reasonably expect to:
    a. get insight into one or two leadership theories.
    b. apply most of the content with success.
    c. resolve conflicts in their own sections at work.
    d. resolve conflicts in organizational governance.
8. The story about the boy who tried unsuccessfully to repair the radio illustrates that:
    a. people with nondominant personalities can become effective leaders.
    b. successful leadership is enhanced by creativity.
    c. successful leadership depends upon structured training.
    d. leaders cannot be effective without authority.

9. The first task that a leader must accomplish is to inform the subordinates of his or her expectations.
   a.   true
   b.   false

10. Beverly Jacoby's difficulties in leadership stemmed mainly from her problems in technical credibility.
    a.   true
    b.   false

11. According to the philosophy of leadership in the text, Dr. Morrison should have advised Beverly to first rectify the problem with her:
    a.   subordinates
    b.   peers
    c.   superiors
    d.   all of the above

12. The power to lead by intimidation can be effective since a leader's power stems from the ability to direct human resources.
    a.   true
    b.   false

13. Dr. Kramer's case illustrates that a leader can have power without credibility
    a.   true
    b.   false

14. Dr. Kramer and Beverly Jacoby both experienced significant difficulties in the same primary area of credibility.
    a.   true
    b.   false

15. Effective leadership will consider the human needs of the workforce without compromising the bottom-line needs of the organization.
    a.   true
    b.   false

16. A work team is considered stable only when the prospects of additional jolts have been eliminated.
    a.   true
    b.   false

17. Which is not a part of the personality?
    a.   id
    b.   hypoego
    c.   superego
    d.   ego

18. The superego relieves the body's pain by stimulating critical thinking.
    a.   true
    b.   false

19. The primary function of the id is to provide self-satisfaction.
    a.   true
    b.   false

20. Following the urge to respond impulsively, the id floods the ego with anxiety.
    a. true
    b. false
21. The superego inhibits the id by working through the ego.
    a. true
    b. false
22. Parents teach their children to inhibit urges and impulses by triggering their children's superego.
    a. true
    b. false
23. When standing in front of a candy machine you perceive an urge to buy a candy bar. A voice inside of you tells you to grow up and develop some will power. The urge comes from the ego, and the advice comes from the superego.
    a. true
    b. false
24. The process of becoming aware that the superego has been triggered is the first step in making a transition into:
    a. the id
    b. the ego
    c. the hypothalamus
    d. none of the above
25. Exercise that increases a muscle's ability to intake and use oxygen is called aerobic:
    a. true
    b. false
26. The process of tensing a muscle, holding the tension, and then abruptly releasing it is called meditative relaxation.
    a. true
    b. false
27. In internal free association, it is important to analyze the thoughts and images in order to reduce the levels of tension that may lead to impulsive power.
    a. true
    b. false
28. The job-list binder is a tool that is used in the management of discretionary time.
    a. true
    b. false
29. Intimidation is most often a form of power without authority.
    a. true
    b. false
30. The relationship life cycle is a model that explains:
    a. the functions within the work team.
    b. the flow of events within a relationship.
    c. the functions within the organization.

    d.   the rules for behavior within relationships.

    e.   none of the above.

31. Emotional maturity is associated most directly with ethical credibility.

    a.   true

    b.   false

32. The formal investigation of a person's credentials is associated with the "credibility" phase of the relationship life cycle.

    a.   true

    b.   false

33. Stability is said to occur when the roles have been clarified and the expectations have been defined.

    a.   true

    b.   false

34. Disintegration follows eroded commitment, with several jolts taking place between the two.

    a.   true

    b.   false

35. Your greatest asset in attempting to establish your credibility is your:

    a.   competence

    b.   recommendations

    c.   integrity

    d.   appearance

    e.   speaking characteristics

36. A door opener is most closely related to which of the following concepts:

    a.   silence

    b.   feedback

    c.   summary

    d.   open-ended question

    e.   active listening

37. When a listener corrects the speaker's understanding, the speaker has likely used which of the following:

    a.   silence

    b.   open-ended question

    c.   feedback

    d.   acknowledgement

    e.   confrontation

38. Assertive behavior seeks self-satisfaction without regard for the other person's welfare.

    a.   true

    b.   false

39. Assertiveness can be distinguished from aggressive confrontation on the basis of self-satisfaction.

    a.   true

    b.   false

40. Match the following relationship styles with their counterparts from the personality:
    ( ) aggressiveness   a. id
    ( ) assertiveness   b. superego
    ( ) nonassertiveness   c. ego
41. The most effective format for agendas is that of a written document.
    a. true
    b. false
42. When workers deviate from the leader's expectations, their actions should be confronted, understood, and modified according to the leader's discretion and prudent judgment.
    a. true
    b. false
43. The most effective means by which to reclarify roles so that stability can be restored is:
    a. managing criticism
    b. arbitration
    c. confrontive criticism
    d. constructive criticism
    e. team problem solving
44. What procedure should be implemented if dysfunctional performance continues after structured negotiation has failed?
    a. arbitration
    b. consequence administration
    c. team problem solving
    d. job termination
    e. defining the problem
45. Effectiveness in leadership is most closely related to which two of the following choices:
    a. skills
    b. personality characteristics
    c. situational variables
    d. physical attributes
    e. genetic predisposition
46. Management and leadership share which of the following functions:
    a. representing the organization to the public
    b. directing human resources
    c. determining organizational purpose
    d. a and c
    e. all of the above
47. By focusing a conversation on the other person, a leader hopes to:
    a. stabilize the superego
    b. access the ego
    c. destabilize the id
    d. all of the above
    e. none of the above

48. Resistance expressed by a subordinate signals that:
    a. the ego has been accessed.
    b. the superego has been triggered.
    c. the ego has been desensitized.
    d. the id has taken control of behavior.
    e. none of the above.
49. In the absence of authority, a leader can only influence subordinates on the basis of interpersonal credibility.
    a. true
    b. false
50. In order to become an effective manager, a person should first have established effectiveness as a leader.
    a. true
    b. false

APPENDIX

APPENDIX A: THE JOB-LIST BINDER FORM
APPENDIX B: THE RESPONSE-TIME BINDER FORM
APPENDIX C: FINAL EXAMINATION—ANSWER KEY

Job-List Binder Form

JOB# _____TITLE _____

INSTRUCTIONS:

Date Scheduled _____ Review Date _____ INT: __

_____

JOB# _____TITLE _____

INSTRUCTIONS:

Date Scheduled _____ Review Date _____ INT: __

_____

JOB# _____TITLE _____

INSTRUCTIONS:

Date Scheduled _____ Review Date _____ INT: __

_____

JOB# _____TITLE _____

INSTRUCTIONS:

Date Scheduled _____ Review Date _____ INT: __

APPENDIX B

Response-Time Binder Form

DATE _____ NAME _____ FILE: _____

BEG. TIME _____ CONTENT:

END TIME: _____

_____

DATE _____ NAME _____ FILE: _____

BEG. TIME _____ CONTENT:

END TIME: _____

_____

DATE _____ NAME _____ FILE: _____

BEG. TIME _____ CONTENT:

END TIME: _____

_____

DATE _____ NAME _____ FILE: _____

BEG. TIME _____ CONTENT:

END TIME: _____

APPENDIX C

Final Examination
Answer Key

1.	e.	28.	a.
2.	a.	29.	b.
3.	a.	30.	b.
4.	a.	31.	a.
5.	a.	32.	a.
6.	b.	33.	a.
7.	a.	34.	a.
8.	c.	35.	a.
9.	b.	36.	d.
10.	b.	37.	c.
11.	a.	38.	b.
12.	b.	39.	b.
13.	b.	40.	(a) aggressiveness
14.	b.		(c) assertiveness
15.	a.		(b) nonassertiveness
16.	b.	41.	a.
17.	b.	42.	a.
18.	b.	43.	e.
19.	a.	44.	b.
20.	b.	45.	a.
21.	a.		c.
22.	a.	46.	b.
23.	b.	47.	b.
24.	b.	48.	d.
25.	a.	49.	b.
26.	b.	50.	b.
27.	b.		

REFERENCES

BACH, G. R., & GOLDBERG, H. (1975). *Creative aggression—The art of assertive living* (pp. 304–318). New York: Avon.

BENJAMIN, A. B. (1969). *The helping interview* (pp. 65–153). Boston: Houghton Mifflin Company.

BOETTINGER, H. M. (1979). *Moving mountains or the art of letting others see things your way.* New York: Collier Macmillan.

BUREAU OF THE CENSUS, U.S. DEPARTMENT OF COMMERCE. (1982–1983). Statistical abstracts of the United States. *National Data Book and Guide to Sources, 1982–1983*, 532–533.

BUSINESS WEEK (1980, November 10). What are they teaching in the B–schools? pp. 61–69.

CARNEGIE, D. (1977). *The quick and easy way to effective speaking.* New York: Pocket Books.

COOPER, K. H. (1972). *The new aerobics.* New York: Bantam.

———— . (1977). *The aerobics way.* New York: Bantam.

DRUCKER, P. (1973). *Management: Tasks, responsibilities, and practices.* New York: Harper and Row.

GORDON, R. A., & HOWELL, J. E. (1959). *Higher education for business.* New York: Columbia University Press.

GORDON, T. (1978). *Leader effectiveness training.* Solana Beach, CA: Effectiveness Training Press.

HALL, C. (1954). *A primer of Freudian psychology*. New York: Mentor.

HOY, F., & BOULTON, W. R. (1983). Problem–solving styles of students: Are educators producing what businesses need? *Collegiate News and Views, 36*, 15–21.

HUNSAKER, P. A., & ALLESSANDRA, A. J. (1980). *The art of managing people*. Englewood Cliffs, NJ: Prentice–Hall, Inc.

JACOBSON, E. (1962). *You must relax*. New York: McGraw–Hill.

LEVINSON, H., & ROSENTHAL, S. (1984). *Corporate leadership in action* (pp. 252–291). New York: Basic Books.

LIVINGSTON, J. S. (1971). The myth of the well–educated manager. *Harvard Business Review*, Jan.–Feb., 79–87.

MAHMOUD, S., & FRAMPTON, C. (1975). An evaluation of management curricula in American Association of Collegiate Schools of Business. *Academy of Management Journal, 18*, 407–411.

MASLOW, A. (1954). *Motivation and personality*. New York: Harper & Row.

McCALL, M. W., & LOMBARDO, M. M. (1983, February). What makes a top executive? *Psychology Today*, pp. 26–31.

McCLELLAND, D. (1975). *Power—The inner experience* (p. 260). New York: Irvington.

McKEAN, K. (1985, February). In search of the unconscious mind. *Discovery*, pp. 12–18.

MIRKIN, G., & HOFFMAN, M. (1978). *The sports medicine book* (pp. 17–18). Boston: Little, Brown.

NEWSWEEK (1983, February 7). The mysteries of the brain. pp. 40–49.

NIERENBERG, G. (1973). *Fundamentals of negotiating*. New York: Hawthorn Books.

PAPEZ, J. (1937). A proposed mechanism of emotion. *Archives of Neurology and Psychiatry, 38*, 725–743.

PETER, T., & WATERMAN, R. (1972). *In search of excellence*. New York: Harper & Row.

POLLACK, J. A., ET AL. (1983). Executives: Perceptions of the future MBA programs. *Collegiate News and Views, 36*, 23–25.

PRENTICE, M.P. (1983). An empirical search for a relevant management curriculum. *Collegiate News and Views*, Winter, 25–29.

REIK, T. (1948). *Listening with the third ear*. New York: Harcourt Brace Jovanovich.

SAGER, A. (1974) *Speech at a glance*. Topsfield, MA: Sager.

SARNOFF, D. (1981). *Making the most of your best*. New York: Doubleday.

————— . (1982). Speech can change your life. New York: Dell.

SMITH, L. (1976). *Improving your child's behavior chemistry* (pp. 40–57). New York: Pocket Books.

STODGILL, R. (1974). *Handbook of leadership: A survey of theory and research*. New York: Free Press. As cited in Yukl, G., *Leadership in organizations* (p. 69).

WAREHAM, J. (1980). *Secrets of a corporate headhunter* (pp. 164–186). New York: Atheneum.

WEBER, R. (1980). *Time is money—The key to managerial success* (p. 46). New York: The Free Press; a division of Macmillan Publishing Company.

WILCOX, M.J. (1983). *Aphasia: Pragmatic considerations. Topics in Language Disorders Journal,* 3(4), 35–48.

WILSON, C. (1979). *The managerial task cycle—A course on the productive management of people and work.* New Canaan, CT: Wilson.

YUKL, G. (1981). *Leadership in organizations.* Englewood Cliffs, NJ: Prentice–Hall, Inc.

INDEX

A

Accountable, 13
Acquainted, 27
Action plan, 117, 121
Active listening, 82, 92
Adaptation to change, 39
Aerobic, 73
Aerobic exercise, 74
Agenda, 103
  formal, 104
  informal, 106
Aggression, 45, 164
Anxiety, 47, 76
  flooding the ego with, 47
Arbitration, 115
Arrivers, 18, 19
Assertiveness, 85
Attachments, 28

Authority, 2, 4, 11, 12, 13
  defined, 6
  recognition as, 7, 158

B

Bach, G., and Goldberg, H., 88, 89
Balance, 42, 43
Becoming acquainted, 27
Behavior operating system, 25, 42,
          133, 143, 151
Benjamin, A., 91
Binders, yearly storage, 89
Biological, 45, 46
Boettinger, H., 109
Brain, 46
Brainstorming, 118, 119
Bureau of the Census, 4

Business:
 failures, 4, 158
 school, 14
 week, 4

C

Carnegie, D., 109
Case studies:
 Beverly Jacoby, 126
  problem, 139-42
  solution, 142-47
 Dr. Kramer, 60-66
 domestic conflict, 49-54
 Jerry Williams, 126
  problem, 147-51
  solution, 151-54
 Mike and Kathy, 49-54
 Mrs. Collins, 26-39
 owner vs. manager, 26-39
 Tom Demerist, 126
  problem, 127-33
  solution, 133-38
Catalyst, 45
Chemistry, brain, 46
Chief executive, 13
Chronological, 105
Clarifications, role, 30
Code of Ethics, 9, 11
Commitment, 31
 eroded commitment, 37
Communication skills, 83
 assertiveness, 85
 confrontation, 87
 conversation, 83
 feedback, 92
Community:
 organization, 6
 service, 4
Companionship, 167
Competence:
 increasing, 8
 technical, 7
 without credibility, 7
Compromise, 120, 167
Computer program, 44

Conflict, 26-39, 159
Confrontation, 87
Conscious awareness, 44, 47
Consensus, 120
Consequences for unsatisfactory
          performance, 122
Constructive criticism, 89, 95
Consumer, 9
Control adjustments, 9, 12
 extent, 16
Conversation, 83
 direct approach, 84
 indirect approach, 85
 initiation, 83
 maintenance, 83
 repair, 83
 termination, 83
 turn taking, 83
Cooper, K., 74
Cooperation, 167
Cooperative achievement, 4
Credibility, 2
 defined, 7
 establishing, 26
 ethical, 2, 7, 9, 158
 interpersonal, 2, 7, 11, 12, 159
 Relationship Life Cycle, 26
 technical, 2, 7, 158
 without competence, 7
Crtitcism, 87
 closure, 94
 confrontative, 88, 95
 constructive, 89, 95
 dealing with, 97
 feedback, 92
 giving, 95
 preparation, 88
 procedural guidelines, 95
 response, 90

D

Daily calendar, 67
Day-scheduling binder, 69
Decision-making, 13, 114
 arbitration, 115

team, 116, 117
Decisive function, 5
Defining expectations, 29
Delegating, 9
Depression, 45
Derailers, 18, 19
Desensitizer, superego, 83, 162, 164
Dignity, 163
Directing resources, 5, 8, 12-13
Directions, 110
Directive:
  function, 5, 8
  skills, 8, 9, 12, 13
Discretionary time, 67
  day-scheduling binder, 69
  job-list binder, 67
Disintegration, 39
Dr. Kramer, 60-66
Dr. Mills, 60-66
Domestic conflict (case study), 49-54
Door opener, 91, 120
Drucker, P., 10

E

Eclectic study, 14
Effective speaking, 108-110
Ego, 55, 66, 90, 160
  defined, 43
  time management, 73
Emotional:
  maturity, 60
  stability, 11, 13, 66, 67
  temperature, 166
Energy, 48
Establishing credibility, 26
Ethical:
  credibility, 9, 11
  principles, 9
Ethics:
  Code of, 9
  professional, 10
Executives:
  arrivers, 18, 19
  derailers, 18, 19
Expectations, 29

F

Facilitating work, 8, 12
Failure:
  business, 4
  to communicate (jolts), 33
Fairchild Medical Group, 139
Family, 13
Fatigue, 47
Feedback, obtaining and providing,
  9, 12
Final examination:
  answer key, 181-82
  test, 169-74
Five-year calendar, 69
Flexibility, 18-19
Flooding the ego, 46-47
Forming attachments, 28
Free association, 76
Freud, S., 161
Function:
  decision making, 13
  decisive, 5
  directive, 5
  representative, 6

G

Giving criticism, 87-95
Goal setting and clarification, 8, 12
Good business practice, 10
Gorden and Howell, 4
Gordon, Dr. T., 89, 91, 117

H

Hall, C., 43, 48
Hippocratic Oath, 9
Hobbies, 84
Home base, 78
Homeostasis, 43, 75, 160
Hoy, F. and Boulton, W., 4
Human behavior, 2, 15, 19, 160
Hunsaker and Alessandra, 109
Hypothalamus, 75

I

Id, 44, 66, 90, 160
  defined, 44
Impulses, 5, 45
Impulsive:
  action, 44
  behavior, 44
  energies, 44
  power, 44
  reactions, 44
Incompetent, 7, 9
Individual accomplishment, 4
Individuality, 4
Industry, organization, 6
Inflexible, 18
Inhibit, 44-46
Insensitive, 18
Insights, 5
Instability, 35
Instructions, 110
Integration, 31
Integrity, 19
Internal free association, 76
Interpersonal:
  credibility, 11, 12
  relations, 25-26
  skills, 13
Interruptions, 91, 112
Interview, 59-60
Intimidation, 66
Irrational behavior, 46
Irritable, 46

J

Jacobson, E., 75
Jacoby, Beverly, 126, 139-47
Job-list binder, 68
  form, 177
Jolts, 33, 114, 122
Judgment, 11
Judicious power, 11

K

Knowledge, 6, 7, 8, 10, 13
Kramer, Dr., 60-66

L

Leader, 2
  defined, 4, 13, 158
  experienced, 15
  influence, 15
  new, 15
  poorly prepared, 14, 20
  relate to people, 17
Leadership, 12, 13, 158
  effective, 15, 16, 20, 160, 168
  skills, 2, 17
    traits, 2, 17
    unqualified, 4
  training (*see* Training, leadership)
Levinson, H., and Rosenthal, S., 11,
  13, 17
Listening:
  active, 92
  passive, 90-91
  reflective, 92
Livingston, J., 4
Logic, 43
Lombardo, M., 18
Loneliness, 45

M

McCall, M., and Lombardo, M., 18
McClelland, D., 15
McKean, K., 161
Mahmoud, S., and Frampton, C., 4
Management, 12
Manager, 2
  defined, 4
Managing:
  criticism, 95
  interruptions, 91, 112
Maslow, A., 15
Maturity, 62
Measure, 14
Measuring performance, 8
Meetings, 103-8
Memos, 165
Mike and Kathy (case study), 49-54
Minutes, 104
Mirkin, G., 73, 74
Modeling, 29, 30

Morale, 11
Morrison, Dr. Lawrence, 139-42
Motivating workers, 8, 15
Motivation, 11, 15

N

Nature of power, 11
Nauman, Sally, 139-42
Needs:
  human behavior, 15
  personal, 9
  professional, 9
Negotiations, 29, 120
Newsweek, 44
Niceguy, 163
Nierenberg, G., 15
Nonblameful, 87, 95
Norepinephrine, 73

O

Objectives, 5
Objective thinking, 43
Open-ended question, 90-91
Organization, 13
  defined, 4
  objectives, 5, 8
    setting task, 8
  steering the, 5
Organizational:
  behavior, 4
  resources, 4, 6, 12
Organized thinking, 44
Organizing work, 8
Overactive kids, 46
Overview (summary), 158-60

P

Pain, 45-46
Papez, J., 161
Paraphrase, 90-91
Participants, 14
Participation:
  structured, 115
  team, 122

Passive listening, 90-91
Perceived personal attack, 46, 54
Personality characteristics, 14, 16, 43,
    160
  ego, 43
  id, 44
  superego, 46
Personal needs, 9, 165
Peters, T., and Waterman, R., 16
Physical activity, 73
Planning and problem solving, 8
Policies, 111
Pollack, J., 4
Positioning, 59
Power, 5, 9, 12, 14, 159
  buying, 7
  defined, 6
  impulsive, 11
  judicious, 11
  license, 6
  misuse of, 11
  organization's, 12
  permission, 6
Pragmatics, 83
Prentice, 4
Pressure, 60
Pride, 60
Primitive emotions (*see* Id)
Problem solving:
  arbitration, 115
  defined, 116
  mediation, 116
  negotiation, 116
  and planning, 8
  team decision making, 116
Procedural guidelines for:
  announcing policies, 112
  criticism:
    confrontive, 95
    constructive, 95
  formal agenda, 105
  giving directions, 111
  informal agenda, 107
  managing interruptions, 114
  team decision making, 122
  unsatisfactory performance,
      consequences, 123
Productive channels, 43
Professional:
  conduct, 9

Professional (*cont.*):
  ethic, 10
  needs, 9
Professors, 14
Progressive relaxation, 75
Public image, 59

Q

Questions:
  closed-ended, 90-91
  open-ended, 90-91
Questions and answers, 160-68
Quick sugars, 46
Quiet time, 76

R

Rational thinking, 46
Reason, 11
Rebound hypoglycemia, 47
Rechannelled energies, 91
Records, 67-73
Reference:
  feeling, 88-95
  nonblameful, 88-95
  problem, 88-95
Reflective listening, 82, 92
  regulated sleep, 75-78
Relationship Life Cycle, 25, 133, 142,
        151, 159
Relationships:
  leader's, 15
  working, 25, 159
Relaxation, 75
Repression, 47
Reprimand, 87-97
Research, 14
Resentment, 46
Resistance, 161
Resources:
  human, 5, 6
  organizational, 5
Response time, 70
  binder, 71
  defined, 70
  form, 179

Results, assessing, 121
Resume, 59
Retrieval:
  categorical, 73
  chronological, 72
Rigidity, 18
Role clarifications, 29
Ruskin, J., 60

S

Sager, A., 108
Sarnoff, D., 109, 110
Self-centered, 44
Self-confidence, 15
Self-esteem, 163
Setting objectives, 8
Shame (*see* Superego)
Silence, 90-91
Simulated experiences, 14
Situational variables, 14
Skills:
  directive, 8, 9, 12, 13
  interpersonal, 13
  leadership, 2
  people, 16
  power, 7
  speaking, 108-10
  specialty, 8, 13
Sleep, 75-78
Smith, L., 46
Society, organization, 6
Speaking before a group, 108-10
Sports Medicine Book, 73-74
Stability:
  emotional, 11, 13, 66, 67, 163
  Relationship Life Cycle, 32
Standards, 9-11
Stodgill, R., 17
Storage binders, 89
Stress (*see* Superego, trigger)
Superego, 46
  anxiety, 47, 54, 67
  attacks, 54
  defined, 46
  desensitizers, 83, 164
  trigger, 54, 66, 67, 83, 160, 164

Supervisor, 2
Survive, 43

T

Team decision making, 116
   analyzing proposal, 120
   assessing the results, 121
   choosing a solution, 121
   defining problem, 117
   determining an action plan, 121
   proposing solution, 118
Technical competence, 9, 11
   defined, 7
   specialty skills, 8
Technical credibility, 9, 11
   defined, 7
Temperament, 164
Temptations, 42
Tension, 11, 76
   level, 11
Thinking:
   objective, 10
   rational, 46
Time management:
   daily calendar, 67
   discretionary time, 67
   response time, 70
   technical competence, 8-9
To-do list, 68
Train, 2
Trainer, 15
Training, leadership, 2
   business seminar, 14
   college level, 14
   structured, 14, 15 159

Traits, leadership, 2
Turn taking, 83

U

Unethical, 9, 163
Urges, 45

V

Ventilate (*see* Superego,
                     desensitizers)
Voice:
   meetings, 103-8
   speaking, 108-10, 163
Vulnerable, 159 (*see also* Superego)

W

Wareham, J., 59
Waterman, R., and Peters, T., 16
Weber, 60, 67
Wilcox, M., 83
Williams, Jerry, 126, 147-54
Wilson, C., 8, 12
Wisdom, 5
Work facilitation, 8
Work team, 11

Y

Yearly storage binders, 89
Yukl, G., 14, 17, 25